Teachers, Students and the Law

A quick reference guide for Australian teachers

5th Edition

Vivien Millane

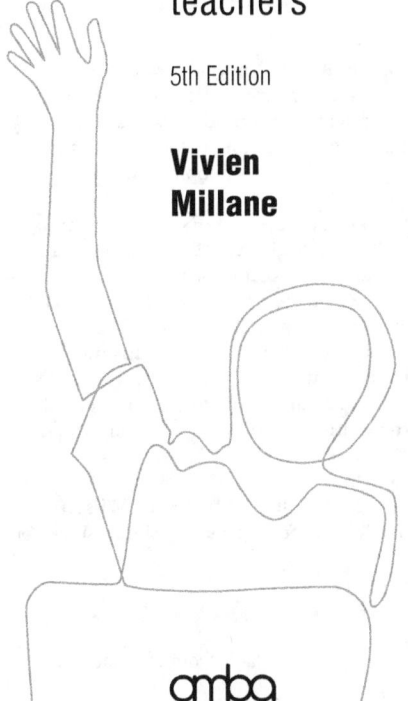

amba press

Published in 2025 by Amba Press, Melbourne, Australia
www.ambapress.com.au

First, first national, second and third editions published 2000,
2002, 2005, 2008 by the Victoria Law Foundation
Fourth edition published 2014 by ACER Press
Fifth edition published 2021 by ACER Press, an imprint of
Australian Council for Educational Research Ltd

© Vivien Millane 2025

In the spirit of reconciliation, Amba Press acknowledges the
Traditional Custodians of country throughout Australia and
their connections to land, sea and community. We pay our
respect to their elders past and present and extend that respect to
all Aboriginal and Torres Strait Islander peoples today.

This book is copyright. All rights reserved. Except under the
conditions described in the Copyright Act 1968 of Australia and
subsequent amendments, and any exceptions permitted under
the current statutory licence scheme administered by Copyright
Agency (www.copyright.com.au), no part of this publication
may be reproduced, stored in a retrieval system, transmitted,
broadcast or communicated in any form or by any means,
optical, digital, electronic, mechanical, photocopying, recording
or otherwise, without the written permission of the publisher.

Edited by Shaneen Goodwin
Cover design, text design and typesetting by Karen Wilson
Cover image © DODOMO, Blinx & Singleline @ shutterstock.com

ISBN: 9781923569188 (pbk)
ISBN: 9781923569195 (ebk)

A catalogue record for this book is available from the National
Library of Australia.

FOREWORD

Schools are communities, and inevitably share many of the same challenges that arise whenever people come together for a common purpose. The law plays a part in guiding group interactions – in workplaces, clubs, and neighbourhoods – but tends to emerge explicitly only when things go awry or a dispute starts.

But schools bring large numbers of children, with diverse backgrounds and needs, together in one place for their academic, social and personal development. While the culture of any particular school will be distinctive, even the happiest and most successful is still a uniquely complex environment. A sound awareness of legal responsibilities and rights can help teachers and principals navigate the very special challenges that come from working with and caring for young people.

ACER Press is to be congratulated on the production of this fine resource authored by Vivien Millane. It provides teachers with a highly accessible guide to the key areas of legal regulation affecting their work and students' experience. I particularly note the timely inclusion in this latest edition of the serious impact of the COVID pandemic upon the educational landscape and which the nation's teachers have worked with such great versatility and professionalism to overcome.

Professor Andrew Lynch
Acting Dean
Faculty of Law & Justice
UNSW Sydney

CONTENTS

Foreword	iii
Using this book	vii

PART 1: Duty of care

Teacher registration and professional standards	2
Duty of care	5
Excursions and camps	25
Non-teaching staff and trainees	32
Volunteers	35
First aid and disease	38
Pandemics	45

PART 2: Discipline, physical contact and relations with students

Student discipline and restraint	52
Physical contact and sexual assault	65
Bullying, harassment and assault	72

PART 3: Provision of educational services

Discrimination	82
Confidentiality, privacy and freedom of information	95
Defamation	103
Professional negligence	109
Copyright	112

PART 4: Welfare, family and crime

Reporting child abuse	126
Family law problems	134
Police interviewing of students	140
Appearing in court	144
Trespass on school property	146
Notes	151
Further reading	155
Directory	157
Index	165

USING THIS BOOK

This book is a plain language guide written for teachers to give you a general explanation of the main areas of law relevant to the teacher–student relationship. Many of the topic areas will also be pertinent to non-teaching staff in schools.

The book answers many common questions about legal issues that concern teachers, and through the case studies and the checklists at the end of each section, it will help you plan your actions to comply with the law. It also indicates where to go for more detailed advice. The 'Directory' section lists further references and some helpful organisations.

This book cannot provide a definitive answer to every legal problem you may confront, as the law is too vast to be covered in one small book. Where terms such as 'reasonableness' and 'due care' are used, precise definitions are not possible as their meaning depends on all the surrounding circumstances. Furthermore, some areas of law are so complex that 'black and white' answers are not always possible. In difficult cases, only a court can ultimately decide, after considering all the relevant facts, whether the law has been broken.

The focus of the book is the teacher–student relationship. For advice on legal issues relating to the employer–employee relationship, you should consult your union or a solicitor. While the book is not directed at school administrators, they should find it a helpful source of information on some of the important issues relevant to them.

The government departments responsible for administering education systems in the states and territories have a variety of names, so, for convenience each is referred to simply as 'the education department' or 'the department'.

PART 1

Duty of care

TEACHER REGISTRATION AND PROFESSIONAL STANDARDS

If you are seeking to work as a teacher in schools in Australia, you must be registered or accredited with your state or territory registration or accreditation authority. Since October 2011, there has been a movement towards a national approach to teacher registration and accreditation under the guidance of the Australian Institute for Teaching and School Leadership (AITSL). AITSL is a public company limited by guarantee, funded by the federal government with the object of providing national leadership for the federal, state and territory governments 'in promoting excellence in the profession of teaching and school leadership'. Teachers beginning the registration process from 1 January 2013 do so under the Australian Professional Standards for Teachers. Each jurisdiction is developing transitional arrangements that will be in place until the nationally consistent registration process is finalised.

Under the national approach, to become a fully registered teacher and to maintain registration, you must not only be qualified academically according to the standards set by your state but you must also demonstrate that you are functioning at or above the proficiency level of the Australian Professional Standards for Teachers and that you are a suitable person to work with children and to be a teacher.

Suitability will be assessed having regard to:
- a criminal record check (CRC)
- a working with children check (WWCC)
- any other relevant information regarding a person's fitness to teach.

CRCs are governed by state legislation. Generally, CRCs must be conducted periodically, usually once every two to five years. The CRC may be conducted separately from the WWCC or conducted at the same time depending on the requirements of each state. Where a CRC reveals an offence that is not relevant to you being able to perform your professional duties as a teacher and you are otherwise of good character and professional standing, you may be able to retain your registration or accreditation.

In general, you may cease to be registered (or, in New South Wales, lose your accreditation) if you:
- do not meet the required standard of professional behaviour
- do not meet the standard of professional performance
- neglect to update your criminal record check or equivalent
- fail to keep your WWCC registration up-to-date
- neglect to pay your annual registration fee.

It is generally an offence for a person who is not registered or accredited as a teacher with the relevant institute to work as a teacher in an Australian school. It is an offence for a school to employ a person to work as a teacher in an Australian school if that person is not registered or accredited.

As a registered teacher in an Australian school, you are required to comply with professional regulatory requirements, relevant federal and state legislation, ministerial guidelines as appropriate and duties under the common law. State and territory teacher registration authorities also have codes of conduct or professional practice that you should familiarise yourself with.

For more details of transitional arrangements, teacher registration or accreditation requirements (including provisional registration/accreditation, English language proficiency and permission to teach) contact the regulatory authority in your state or territory.

Australian Capital Territory Teacher Quality Institute
www.tqi.act.edu.au

New South Wales Education Standards Authority
www.educationstandards.nsw.edu.au

Teacher Registration Board of the Northern Territory
www.trb.nt.gov.au

Queensland College of Teachers
www.qct.edu.au

Teachers Registration Board of South Australia
www.trb.sa.edu.au

Teachers Registration Board of Tasmania
www.trb.tas.gov.au

Victorian Institute of Teaching
www.vit.vic.edu.au

Teacher Registration Board of Western Australia
www.trb.wa.gov.au

See also:

Australian Institute for Teaching and School Leadership
www.aitsl.edu.au

DUTY OF CARE

Duty of care at common law goes back to the early years of the twentieth century and is an element of the tort of negligence. (A tort is a wrong that results in injury to another person, for which they can seek compensation; a civil wrong.) Being judge-made law, it is being constantly developed and updated as new cases come before the courts. Social change and advances in technology require judges to interpret the law in light of new circumstances so that, although the principles remain the same, the application of those principles expands to meet the demands of each new generation.

What are those principles? In order for a claim in negligence to succeed, the plaintiff must show that:
- the defendant owed a duty of care to the plaintiff
- the defendant breached the duty of care
- the risk of injury was foreseeable
- the risk was not insignificant (i.e. it was more likely than not to happen)
- the injury was caused by the breach of the duty of care.

The teacher's duty of care

The law regards the teacher–student relationship as having a special welfare component. This special teacher–student relationship arose when compulsory education was introduced. When the state took responsibility for the education of children, those children of school age were removed from the control of their parents and placed under the authority and control of the education department. Schools and teachers took on the authority of the parent and duty of care for the child (in loco parentis). However, as the law developed, the duty of care expected of the teacher took on a higher standard than that expected of a parent. The standard of care expected of you, the teacher, today is that of a 'reasonable teacher'. This means that you have a 'duty of care' to protect your students from reasonably foreseeable injuries. This standard takes into account that you have been trained in the care and management of children and have reached a level of professional expertise.

The courts recognise that accidents happen in schools, and you will have breached your duty of care only if:
- the injury was reasonably foreseeable, i.e. not completely unexpected, AND
- the injury occurred because you did not carry out your responsibilities in a sufficiently careful manner.

There is no clear-cut definition of terms like 'reasonable' or 'careful'. Whether the duty of care has been broken depends on the particular facts of each case. For example, teachers on yard duty would not be responsible for a sudden, unforeseeable attack by one student on another. However, you could be implicated if you had failed to do, or were late for, your rostered yard duty and, as a result, no teacher was present to deal with a student fight.

The duty of care also requires you to be proactive where students could be injured. For example, if you are crossing the schoolyard and encounter students behaving dangerously, you should intervene even if you are not on official yard duty. However, in circumstances where it is foreseeable that physical intervention could result in injury to you or to others, you should send for help and rely on voice control until assistance arrives (see 'Restraint', p. 54).

Teachers who act carefully and sensibly, and plan and supervise activities properly, should not fear being sued for injuries suffered by students.

Legal protection for employees

At common law, employers are vicariously liable for the negligent acts of their employees done in the course of their employment. This means that the school rather than the teacher would be held liable for damages arising from the negligent acts of a teacher that were expressly or impliedly authorised by the school, or were clearly within the scope of employment.

Additional statutory protection has been provided to employees in New South Wales, South Australia and the Northern Territory. In New South Wales, protection against claims in negligence exists for employees pursuant to the *Employees Liability Act 1991*. Under this legislation an employee is not personally liable for a tort if an employer is also liable for that tort, and the employee has a right to be indemnified by the employer if the employee is sued. This protection only applies to conduct in the course of employment and arising out of employment and does not apply to serious or wilful misconduct by the employee. Similar protections are available to employees in South Australia under the *Civil Liability Act 1936* and in the Northern Territory under the *Law Reform (Miscellaneous Provisions) Act 1956*.

Furthermore, this legal protection will not be relevant to disciplinary matters or reputation damage in the rare circumstances where the conduct of the employee does not amount to misconduct but is seen as at least partly to blame for injury suffered by a child.

The school's duty of care

The school's duty of care is broader than a teacher's and includes:
- adequate supervision of students
- protecting students from dangerous situations and activities
- maintaining safe premises and equipment

- providing a safe, supportive and productive learning environment when students are studying online
- protecting students from bullying and excessively rough play by other students (see 'Bullying, harassment and assault', p. 72).

The school's duty of care to the teacher

The school has a duty of care to the teacher to provide a safe workplace and a safe teaching environment. In a recent case in the Victorian Supreme Court[1] a teacher was awarded over $1.2 million in damages, having developed severe mental health issues resulting from a heavy and unbalanced workload over a number of years. The court held that the school was in breach of its duty of care to the teacher. The school was aware of the difficulties the teacher was facing but ignored his deteriorating mental health, continuing to allocate him a teaching load heavily weighted with difficult classes, which were described in the court as 'feral' and failed to provide monitoring and support. The risk of a mental breakdown was foreseeable.

Work stress is not itself an indicator that a teacher is likely to suffer a serious mental breakdown. The teacher must bring the threat to their mental health to the attention of the school and request support. If the school is not aware of the problem, the school can argue that the risk of injury was not foreseeable.

It is also foreseeable that students allocated to classes known to be 'difficult' or 'feral' could be disadvantaged and the school could be in breach of its duty to those students unless provision was made for intervention, monitoring and additional support.

Non-government schools

Non-government schools and teachers have the same duty of care as government schools and teachers. Although education department guidelines on safety issues are not binding on non-government schools, they are a useful indicator of what is expected and can be used by these schools in drafting their own policies.

When is the duty of care owed?

Schools and teachers have a duty of care to students whenever the school is exercising control over the students' actions. This includes:

- anywhere curricula or co-curricula activities are taking place, i.e. in classrooms, laboratories, computer rooms, gymnasiums, libraries, etc. This now includes online activities
- in outdoor and indoor play areas
- before and after school hours where pupils are allowed to enter school property, or in situations where the principal has knowledge that the students are congregating before or after school creating a foreseeable risk of injury
- during sport and physical education activities
- when students are moving about the school
- on transport arranged by the school, or on public transport where the principal has knowledge that there is a serious risk of bullying or other danger
- when students are travelling for or playing school sport away from the school
- during excursions and school camps (see 'Excursions and camps', p. 25)
- after school, including in the home environment, where the principal or teacher has knowledge that the student is being subjected to cyberbullying.

The duty is owed throughout the whole school day (and 24 hours a day in boarding schools). Generally schools are not responsible when students are travelling to or from school on public transport. An exception could arise where the school or teacher knew of some danger to students, or knew of a danger that a student might pose to the public, and failed to provide a warning about it. A duty may arise at the bus stop, tram stop or train station near school (see 'Before and after school', below).

The general rule is that the duty of care is no longer owed once you have finished duties for the day and gone home. However, the growth of online activity is blurring the boundaries between school and home.

Before and after school

Court cases have decided that the duty of care can arise before school, but they have not indicated a precise starting time for this duty. Courts have also ruled that the duty can extend beyond the school gate before and after school, but they have not indicated how far from the school gate it extends, and for how long.

Courts have, however, made it clear that once the school asserts authority over students (such as by making rules about behaviour in the playground before school, setting supervision times or supervising a bus stop) then the duty of care has arisen. Adequate supervision should then be provided (see 'Playground supervision', p. 20).

The point at which the duty of care arises depends entirely on the circumstances—for example, the age and numbers of children who arrive early at school, the sorts of activities they engage in and the known general behaviour of the students.

In one case, a court found that the school should have provided supervision for primary school students at a bus stop 300 metres from the school.[2] In another case, a court found that the school should have attempted to supervise Year 12 students who were misbehaving outside the school gate on their end-of-year 'muck up' day.[3] In a 1977 case, the High Court found a school liable for an injury that occurred in the playground 10 minutes before playground supervision began and 35 minutes before school began, because the school had asserted control over student behaviour.[4]

In a 2006 New South Wales case, the court found that a school playground should have been supervised at 8.10 am when a boy was injured. The school bell did not ring until 8.35 am, but the school had been accepting students from about 8.00 am onwards.[5]

Each school should adopt a supervision policy appropriate to its own circumstances and communicate it to parents. You should comply with the policy (see 'Who is liable? The teacher or the school?', p. 12). The policy should explain the supervision provided before and after school and at public transport stops and stations.

Online learning activities

The digital learning environment extends beyond the boundaries of the traditional classroom and the traditional school day. With the delivery of curriculum through online learning, in circumstances where the student is confined to home, your duty of care has been extended into the home environment (see 'Pandemics', p. 45). It is not reasonable to expect a principal or teacher to monitor every site or expect them to supervise online activity 24 hours a day. However, where online learning has replaced onsite learning, or, has even supplemented it, you have a duty to see that the student is learning in the home environment and that the technology is as safe as possible, is appropriate for the task and is being used appropriately. In general, a principal cannot exercise control over the child in the home environment, but where teaching has been transferred from the onsite classroom to in-home learning it is reasonable to expect that the school provides reasonable supervision (see 'Online courses and the duty of care', p. 47). In any event, the principal or teacher should respond to an online incident as soon as they know about it, particularly if the perpetrator is a member of the school community. If the perpetrator is anonymous, or if the incident involves possible criminal activity, the police may need to be informed to protect the health and safety of the students (see 'Grooming a child under 16', p. 68; 'Cyberbullying', p. 75; 'Keeping students safe in a digitised world', p. 76).

School events

Schools should have a policy on what is and is not a 'school event'. Consider the following examples:

- A school 'formal' or social function organised by parents for students. If the school does not intend this to be an official school occasion, it should advise parents and students accordingly, and take no part in the organisation of the function. It should also advise the organising parents to ensure that appropriate public liability insurance covers the function. If it is an official school event, or the school is involved in its organisation, then a duty of care will arise, and adequate supervision of the students should be provided.
- Use of school grounds outside of school hours, by an external body such as a sporting association, for activities not organised by the school. The school must ensure that premises and equipment such as goal rings are in a safe condition, and should warn of any risks that are not obvious.

Who is liable? The teacher or the school?

A school's duty of care cannot be delegated to anyone else. Even if an injury is caused by a teacher's carelessness, the school will still be liable. When a student is injured, the parents are more likely to sue the school than the teacher, as the school's insurance policy will pay the compensation for the injuries. If the case goes to court, however, the teacher might be called as a witness (see 'Appearing in court', p. 144). Nevertheless, a major concern for teachers is the protection of their reputation, and there is no guarantee—except in New South Wales, South Australia and the Northern Territory—that your school or the education department will cover you if you are sued (see 'What to do if you are sued', p. 14). If you are teaching in a government school, you should check the department's policy regarding indemnifying you for injuries you may cause to others. A school is less likely to be liable for students' injuries where a teacher has acted in a criminal manner, and the school's carelessness has not contributed to the commission of the crime.

The school will also not be liable where teachers are seen to be acting in a private capacity. For example, if you took students on a weekend canoeing excursion or to a film after school, without school approval, you might be liable if your carelessness contributed to students' injuries. Furthermore, such conduct could open you to suspicion of 'grooming' or, at the very least, be seen as inappropriate (see 'Physical contact and sexual assault', p. 65). In these circumstances, the protection that exists for employees under the common law and legislation in New South Wales, South Australia and the Northern Territory would not apply. Accordingly, full details of any extra activities should be provided to the school and official written approval obtained, together with written consent from the parents (see 'Excursions and camps', p. 25). You must establish clear boundaries between your professional and personal lives and avoid any activities that could blur these boundaries.

It is also important to note that health and safety legislation imposes an obligation on all employees (not just teachers) to take reasonable care for the health and safety of persons who may be affected by the employee's acts or omissions at a workplace. Accordingly, very careless acts, for example in a science laboratory, could lead to prosecution. This is a separate legal proceeding from a student suing the school for breach of the duty of care.

Work Health and Safety Act 2011 (WHS) is the national harmonised law, which has been legislated in all states and territories except Victoria and Western Australia. The *Occupational Health and Safety Act 2004* (OHS) still applies in Victoria and the Victorian government has indicated that it has no intention of legislating the WHS. Western Australia has indicated that it intends to legislate the WHS but has not yet done so. Western Australia still operates under its *Occupational Safety and Health Act 1984* (OSH). Whichever legislation is in force, the obligation for an employee to take reasonable care for the health and safety of others in the workplace remains the same and teachers must take reasonable care for their own safety, for that of other workers and for their students.

What to do if you are sued

Where a student is suing the school for injuries suffered, teachers can also be named as defendants (persons being sued). If this happens to you, you should seek legal advice from your union or a solicitor.

Theoretically it is possible that your employer might provide lawyers to act on your behalf or might pay your costs or damages, but it would be more common that the legal representatives for the school would offer to represent you as well. This is sometimes preferable to having your own representation (provided you discuss the issues carefully with the school's solicitor) as this reduces the chance of a conflict developing between you and the school and also will not involve you in any cost. If you think there may be a conflict of interest with your employer, ensure you are clear about the nature of the conflict and seek independent legal advice (for legal help, see 'Directory', p. 157).

How careful do you have to be?

The courts expect teachers to act as carefully as a 'reasonable' teacher would. How careful this should be depends on all the circumstances. For example, in one case, a teacher absent from her class was found not to have been careless

Duty of care

when a student pushed another student off a chair. The court found that the student's behaviour was unpredictable, given that it was a generally well-behaved class, and that the incident could still have occurred if the teacher had remained in the room.[6] On the other hand, there have been cases where teachers have been found to be careless because, although they were in the classroom, they did not take steps to stop students' rough play.

A court will consider the following matters when deciding whether sufficient care has been exercised.

Was that particular event foreseeable?

The court will determine first whether the event was reasonably foreseeable, or whether such a risk was insignificant or too far-fetched. For example, in a case where a student was injured by a catapulted ballpoint pen, the court held that the teacher had exercised adequate supervision. She had instructed the students to put the catapults in the bin and had reasonably believed that they had done so. The class was not known for misbehaviour and the injury was not reasonably foreseeable.[7] In another case, a court found that it was foreseeable that adolescent boys would swing on an unlocked flagpole halyard.[8]

Courts have indicated that a school's duty of care could include protecting students from sunburn. It is advisable to adopt 'sunsmart' strategies, such as hats for outdoor play.

An injury can be more foreseeable in particular circumstances, for example, bad weather, on a total fire ban day, or if old or faulty equipment is being used.

Obviously it is more foreseeable that an injury will occur if a teacher is out of the classroom. Accordingly, you should only leave the class if it is absolutely necessary and this necessity outweighs the risk of any injury occurring.

When a court has decided that a risk was reasonably foreseeable, it will take into account the following sorts of matters to decide whether the teacher has taken the precautions a 'reasonable' teacher would have taken.

The age and capacity of the students
Injuries might be foreseeable because of the age and capacity of the students, for example, a barbecue can be a hazard for very young children, but not for Year 12s. You should be aware of the range of capacities within an age group. Students with special education needs or physical disabilities may require special care.

The behaviour of the group or individual
Classes or individuals who are known to behave badly should be supervised more carefully than students known to be generally well behaved. If you are new to a school or relieving, you should be informed of known difficulties. The school should also inform you about any students with known behavioural problems that could threaten the safety of staff or other students (see 'Restraint', p. 54).

Weighing the risk against the likelihood of it occurring
Even though a risk is foreseeable, a teacher or school will not be held liable where, after weighing the likelihood of injury against the expense of removing the risk, the court finds that adequate care was taken.

For example, most playground risks would be eliminated if most of the staff were on duty there all the time. This is impractical and, accordingly, courts only require 'reasonable' supervision of the playground (see 'Playground supervision', p. 20).

The gravity of the risk
Greater care has to be taken in a science class where chemicals are being used than, say, in a class where students are watching a film. Similarly, an activity like abseiling

requires greater care in its organisation and supervision than tennis.

Can the risk be justified on educational grounds?

The courts recognise that many educational activities involve some risk of injury, and accept the risk if it is in pursuit of a worthwhile educational objective. However, the court may make recommendations, which schools and teachers should be aware of. For example, when two students died on separate ski trips in New South Wales in 2009, the coroner, while recognising the valuable contribution ski excursions can make to the acquisition of physical skill, knowledge and personal development, made recommendations with respect to supervision and management of students on ski excursions to further minimise the risk.[9]

Contact sports such as Australian Rules football or rugby matches have a foreseeable level of risk that must be managed carefully. However, a game played fairly and in accordance with the rules and guidelines will not normally breach the duty of care. But it could be carelessness where very young students are allowed to play a contact sport with much bigger, older students.

Similarly, in science classes it is important that students have the opportunity to experiment, provided that it is accompanied by safety instructions and proper supervision.

When students use the internet there is a risk that they may obtain sexually explicit material and be exposed to other dangerous elements. With the increased popularity of social media sites and schools adopting 'bring your own device' (BYOD) policies, the digital learning environment extends well beyond the traditional school day. You should provide adequate supervision and restrict access to inappropriate sites during school activities. Schools should provide students with training on how to safely use social media and how to protect themselves from unwanted behaviour online (see 'Cyberbullying', p. 75; 'Sexting', p. 60). At a

minimum, the school should have in place internet policies that cover the following areas:
- acceptable use of technology
- social media
- bullying
- privacy.

Common practice and accepted professional standards

If you are complying with common practice based on accepted professional standards, for example, on the sports field or in the gymnasium, then you are probably exercising sufficient care. However, the courts can declare the common practice to be unsafe. Always ask yourself, 'Is injury foreseeable and have I done enough to prevent it?'.

Be aware that professional standards will change in response to increased understanding of the risks involved in school activities. Always attempt to implement best practice. For example, increased data on the long-term effects of concussion and the 2012 Zurich 'Consensus Statement on Concussion in Sport' have resulted in new guidelines for schools and teachers.[10] Concussion should always be taken seriously and schools should have procedures in place, such as removing students with a suspected concussion from play until given medical clearance, to protect the welfare of students. As research improves our knowledge and understanding of sport-related concussion (SRC), schools should develop an SRC policy that is regularly reviewed and updated. For example, the 'Consensus Statement on Concussion in Sport' from the 5th International Conference on Concussion recommends a 10-step return-to-sport-strategy for schools.[11]

If you are asked to teach or supervise students outside your area of expertise, be aware that you may be at risk of breaching professional standards—this is particularly the case in practical classes or sport. If you are required to teach or supervise an activity for which you feel unqualified, check whether there is a school policy on this. If there is no policy, you may wish to contact your union or your solicitor for advice.

Student:teacher ratios and guidelines

Schools (including non-government schools) should follow guidelines from the central educational authority (or develop their own guidelines) for the appropriate ratio of teachers to students on an excursion. You should regard these guidelines as a minimum safety standard. A greater level of supervision than is recommended should be provided if circumstances warrant it, for example, if the activity is dangerous or the group is unskilled. The school should never provide less.

The courts can find that these guidelines are inadequate. For example, in a case where a child died after falling and striking his head during an arduous bush walk, the judge found the student:teacher ratio on the hike to be inadequate, even though it was better than the education department's recommended ratio. The judge took into account the age and limited experience of the students, the weather, and the rugged and remote nature of the terrain.[12]

Teachers with specialist skills

Specialist teachers should exercise the degree of skill expected of a person with their training. For example, science teachers should know which chemicals or experiments are dangerous. Activities that require specialist teacher training should only be carried out by such teachers. When you are filling in for a specialist teacher or are teaching outside of your own area of qualifications, you should limit your activities to what you can safely control and supervise. Schools should have clear policies on this matter.

Weighing up all these considerations

A 2005 High Court case illustrates how courts weigh all these factors to see whether there has been negligence. The court found no breach of the school's duty of care where a Year 3 student was injured when two other students pulled her off a flying fox. At the time there were four teachers supervising the 540 primary school students. The children had been instructed not to touch anyone on the flying fox, and there had been no misbehaviour on the flying fox in the past. An experienced teacher was supervising the activity, and the accident happened in the brief time when her back was turned. All these factors suggested that the probability of injury was slight and did not justify the expense and inconvenience of rostering more teachers on playground duty. The High Court also commented that it is not reasonable to observe children 'every single moment of time' as this retards the development of responsibility in children and is 'damaging to teacher–pupil relationships by removing even the slightest element of trust'.[13]

Playground supervision

The amount of playground supervision required varies according to the age and nature of the student body. Supervision rosters are the responsibility of school administrators, not teachers. The standard of care expected of you while supervising the playground, or organising sport and physical education, is determined by the factors mentioned above (see 'How careful do you have to be?', p. 14).

In one case where a child was injured in the playground, the judge noted that the school occupied a 6.7 hectare site, had 700 students and 60 teachers, and that seven teachers were supervising the playground at the time of the accident. The judge concluded that the school was not in breach of its duty, although 'with hindsight one extra teacher could have been engaged in the relevant area'.[14] (See also the

High Court decision discussed in 'Weighing up all these considerations', p. 20.)

You must know the school's supervision policy, and always carry out rostered supervision. Schools should investigate where bullies operate (see 'Bullying, harassment and assault', p. 72). School policies need to be flexible to accommodate special days, for example, where many students will arrive early.

Sport and physical education

The following are some guidelines for the organisation of sport and physical education:

- Inexperienced students should be more carefully instructed and monitored than experienced students, particularly where the sport is hazardous, e.g. ice skating, trampolining.
- Take special care with low-skilled students, e.g. do not place them in dangerous fielding positions in cricket.
- Do not force students to participate in activities that are beyond their capabilities.
- Supervise contact sports to prevent rough play.
- Small or younger students should not play against larger students where the disparity in size will increase the risk of injury.
- Proper protective clothing or equipment should be compulsory, e.g. mouthguards for hockey, helmets for cricket.
- Safety equipment must be adequate, e.g. sufficient mats for high jump and gymnastic activities.
- Students should be properly instructed about the importance of warm-up exercises or any safety procedures for particular sports.
- Highly dangerous activities, such as abseiling or kayaking, must be carried out with a very high degree of care.

- Do not rely on the recommended student:teacher ratio for a sport if students have a low level of skill or if the weather is poor.
- If you are supervising sport without having any physical education training, school administrators must be sure that you can do the job.
- There must be policy and procedures in place to recognise and manage sport-related concussion (SRC).

If adequate supervision or safety cannot be provided, the activity should not take place.

What to do if a student is injured

The existence of the duty of care requires teachers to take control of emergency situations (see 'First aid and disease', p. 38). Every school should have procedures for dealing with emergencies, and you should familiarise yourself with them. The following are general guidelines:

- Organise medical care for the student as required.
- If concussion is suspected, follow the relevant procedures for concussion.
- Check with the school administration if there are any special instructions from the parents regarding medical care.
- If the accident occurred away from school, try to obtain the names and addresses of any witnesses.
- At the earliest possible opportunity, write a detailed and objective report, recording the chronology of events, witnesses and a brief statement of the circumstances. Record only facts and observations, not opinions, value judgements or assumptions. These notes should be made part of the school's official records, not kept as your private property. (If a case goes to court, it will not be for months, or sometimes years. Detailed notes, made as soon as possible after

the event, will aid recall. The contents of the notes may be revealed in court.)

Injury caused by another student

It is possible for one student to sue another, particularly if an injury is deliberately inflicted. However, the courts do not expect as high a standard of care from students as they do from teachers. Furthermore, the student will usually not have any money to pay compensation. It is more likely that an injured student would sue the school and attempt to show that the injury was caused by a lack of supervision.

A student who has been assaulted by another student may be able to receive financial assistance from their state or territory victims of crime assistance scheme. A teacher injured trying to prevent an assault may also be assisted.

Injured student at fault

Courts can reduce the amount of compensation that a school has to pay to an injured student if the student's own carelessness contributed to the accident.

Apologies

Apologising to a student when an accident has occurred might be an important part of the student's healing process, and may help teachers deal with any guilt they might feel about an accident. The law provides that the giving of an apology that expresses sorrow, regret or sympathy will not in itself amount to an admission of liability.

However, here the law varies from state to state, and it is important that advice from your union or lawyer is taken with regard to the wording of the apology before the apology is given, as some states specify that the apology should not contain an admission of fault.

CHECKLIST

- ☑ Be safety conscious and aware of possible risks in the classroom, in the playground or at sport.
- ☑ Discuss safety issues with colleagues and students, including whether particular students are a safety risk.
- ☑ Consider what children can cope with at particular ages.
- ☑ Obtain school approval and parental consent for all out-of-school activities.
- ☑ Ask yourself, 'Am I acting as the reasonable or careful teacher would in these circumstances?'
- ☑ Question whether the common practice is safe for each particular group of students and the conditions, and if it is in line with written guidelines.
- ☑ Report suspected bullying to the appropriate coordinator or the principal.
- ☑ Always carry out rostered yard duty diligently and arrive promptly for the rostered time.
- ☑ Regard school or department guidelines and student:teacher ratios as a minimum safety standard and insist on higher standards if the group or conditions warrant it.
- ☑ Always use safe equipment.
- ☑ When using external providers, satisfy yourself that those suppliers have the necessary specialist qualifications and safe equipment.
- ☑ Take detailed notes immediately after an incident, and get witnesses' names and addresses, and a statement if possible.

EXCURSIONS AND CAMPS

This section should be read in conjunction with 'Duty of care' (p. 5).

Schools and teachers owe a duty of care to students for the duration of a camp or excursion. This does not mean that you should sit up all night as a 'guard' at a camp, unless there is some foreseeable danger (see 'How careful do you have to be?', p. 14).

In the case of activities such as Duke of Edinburgh overnight walks, make sure that students and parents are aware of how much oversight the school will be exercising. All staff involved in the Duke of Edinburgh scheme should receive very specific training. (See the comments of the coroner in the inquest into the death of David Iredale.[1])

Camps run by other organisations

Schools often take students to camps operated commercially. Those operators are also under a duty to run the camp safely. However, this does not extinguish the school's and teachers' duty of care. You should still satisfy yourself that the camp equipment and activities are safe, and should speak to the camp operators if you believe insufficient care is being taken. If there are difficulties with the operators, or you are unsure what to do, contact the principal or a senior staff member at school.

To fulfil its duty to the students, the school should check that:
- the site run by the external provider is apparently safe

- the equipment is apparently safe
- staff working with the students have current Working With Children Checks (or equivalent)
- the external trainers are competent and possess the specialist qualifications to teach the skills they have been employed to teach.

Even where the school has satisfied itself that the site and activities run by an external provider are apparently safe, the school may still be held responsible for the negligence of the external provider. In a recent case in New South Wales, a student on a school excursion was injured while participating in lessons provided by a ski resort. The court found both the ski resort and the school liable for the student's injury. The court found the ski resort negligent for failing to check for hazards on the beginner's course before commencing the lesson. The school's liability arose from its non-delegable duty of care. However, the court also held that the school was entitled to a full indemnity from the ski resort, since the resort had full control over and responsibility for the site and the activity.[2]

When drafting a contract for external services the school should include an indemnity clause and check that the provider has sufficient current public liability insurance.

Planning camps and excursions and risk assessment

The key to fulfilling your duty of care is to plan thoroughly and keep records of procedures followed. Planning should include the carrying out of a full risk assessment, and the identification of ways to remove or minimise risk. This will include considering the following points.

Know the area

As one of the organising teachers, you must know the environment that students are entering and identify any hazards. Inspect new areas beforehand or make enquiries from past users. For example, check what safety equipment is needed, and what is appropriate clothing and footwear.

When planning a hike, know the nature of the terrain, have current information about the availability of water, identify any possible difficulties and consider whether students have sufficient mental or physical ability to undertake the activity. Consider what instructions will be given to students who may become isolated from the group and whether any students may be at greater risk of this.

Supervision and student:teacher ratios

When organising a camp or excursion, insist on a ratio that you believe is essential for adequate supervision in the circumstances (see 'Student:teacher ratios and guidelines', p. 19). Ensure that it is clear who is in charge and that any volunteers (including parents or other adults) must agree to be directed by that person.

Medical histories and consent

For camps or overnight excursions, each student's parent or guardian should complete a form that:

- provides all relevant information about their child's health—current medication and ailments, previous illnesses or operations, allergies, disabilities, etc. Read this information before the excursion and take it and any required medication with you
- consents to the student receiving all necessary emergency medical treatment, including administering of anaesthetics and the use of an ambulance.

Your risk assessment should include a plan for transporting injured or sick children, and for obtaining emergency medical assistance.

Consent form

A parent or guardian must sign a form consenting to the student's participation, based on full knowledge of what the camp or excursion involves (transport arrangements, planned activities, any potential hazards, safety arrangements and availability of medical assistance for remote locations). Students should not be permitted to go on the excursion without a signed consent form.

Overnight and day excursions in the higher risk category

It is essential that a separate form is signed for every overnight excursion and for day excursions that are perceived to be in a higher risk category. Parents should also be asked to indicate their children's skill level where relevant, for example, if swimming or bike riding is involved.

Forms that attempt to exempt the school from any legal liability for injuries suffered by a child during an excursion are worthless, as courts will not permit parents to sign away a child's right to sue.

Routine day excursions in the lower risk category

In some schools, parents may be asked to sign a generic permission form at the beginning of the year to cover all routine excursions planned for that year. The form must state the type of activities covered (e.g. visits to museums, churches, theatres, libraries) and the mode of transport. A week before an excursion takes place, the parents should be supplied with further details (e.g. educational purpose of the excursion, activities, time of departure, lunch arrangements, time of return). Any parents who have not signed the generic form at the beginning of the year must sign a separate consent form for each excursion, including routine excursions.

You must make sure that you take with you on the excursion the medical information and emergency numbers that parents have supplied to the school.

Excursions and camps

Planning for an emergency

This should be part of the risk assessment carried out before any excursion. Where a remote location is involved, you should devise a plan for dealing with hazards (bushfire, snakebite, etc.) or a medical emergency. An Emergency Position Indicating Radio Beacon (EPIRB) would normally also be desirable. If the group divides, ensure that each subgroup has all necessary emergency information and equipment.

If your state has an online Student Activity Locator (SAL), you should enter activities such as camps and excursions onto the database. Where there are risks to the safety of students and staff from bushfires, floods or other emergencies, the database is used by emergency services to make the authorities aware of your location.

Take a mobile phone that will work in the area, and note the location and phone numbers of police, fire, ambulance and other relevant emergency services. Also carry emergency contact numbers for each child.

Health care and first aid

- A basic first-aid kit is necessary for most excursions.
- At least one adult with first-aid training should accompany an excursion involving physical activity or a remote location.
- If the group breaks into subgroups, each group should have ready access to a trained first aider.
- An adult capable of doing resuscitation should be present if students are swimming.
- During long camps that involve much physical activity, you should check that all students eat adequate meals.

Clothing and weather

- Ensure that students have proper clothing, footwear and sun protection.

- Students with blisters should not be forced to undertake further hikes.
- Monitor how well students cope with extreme weather conditions.
- In case of heavy rain, consider whether flooding of rivers is a possibility, whether there is an alternative route to avoid river crossings and whether the group leaders are aware of the alternative route.
- If the weather deteriorates, consider whether the excursion should be cancelled altogether. If the group has already set out, ensure they can be informed of the changed weather conditions.

Use of your own car

It is not illegal to transport students in your car. However, you are responsible for the behaviour of students travelling as passengers in your car, and it is difficult to supervise students if you are driving. Accordingly, if misbehaviour is likely to be an issue, you should avoid transporting students in your car unless it is an emergency. A further consideration is that a car is a concealed area, so a teacher alone with a student could be vulnerable to allegations of improper conduct in the same way that a teacher in a concealed office or classroom could be (see 'Physical contact and sexual assault', p. 65).

The legal liability for injuries to a student passenger from a car accident is the same as for any other passenger. An injured student can seek compensation under the compulsory third-party insurance scheme in your state or territory.

If you are going to use your own car, you should check with the school beforehand to see if the school will reimburse you for damage to the car or damage your driving may cause to others' property. If not, you will have to meet any expenses. If there are a small number of students it is better to hire a mini-bus.

Excursions and camps

If using your own car to transport students, you must ensure:
- the school knows of and accepts the mode of transport
- parents have given informed consent
- the car is roadworthy
- you will not be alone with one student in the car
- there is adequate supervision given the age, maturity and known behavioural traits of those being transported.

CHECKLIST

- ☑ Plan carefully and keep records of plans and procedures.
- ☑ Carry out a thorough risk assessment before all excursions and camps.
- ☑ Know the excursion area and any hazards.
- ☑ Satisfy yourself that any external providers have the necessary qualifications and that the equipment and site are apparently safe.
- ☑ Ensure that external contractors have adequate current public liability insurance and that the school will be indemnified in the event of an accident caused by the negligence of the contractor.
- ☑ Ensure that all those working with the students have current Working With Children Checks (or equivalent).
- ☑ Be aware of each student's skill level relevant to the activities.
- ☑ Ensure that parents are fully informed about the activities and have consented in writing.
- ☑ Ensure that supervision is adequate for the age and ability of the students.
- ☑ For an overnight excursion, have an emergency plan, a first-aid kit, a mobile phone, students' medical histories and emergency contacts.
- ☑ Monitor students' health and reaction to weather and physical exertion.
- ☑ If using your own car, check that the school will indemnify you for damage.

NON-TEACHING STAFF AND TRAINEES

A school's non-teaching staff can include laboratory technicians, library assistants, computer technicians, integration aides, clerical assistants, gardeners and maintenance staff. Also, trainee teachers, who teach classes under supervision and assist with other activities, will be covered in this section.

Duty of non-teaching staff

Non-teaching staff do not owe the extensive duty of care to students that teachers owe (see 'Duty of care', p. 5). However, as employees, they must carry out their jobs in a safe manner and exercise due care and skill. For example, laboratory technicians must take care when handling equipment and chemicals, or when issuing them to students. A register of hazardous substances must be prepared together with a risk assessment and material safety data sheets (MSDS).

If non-teaching staff see students acting in a dangerous manner, or notice buildings or equipment in a dangerous state, they should report the matter to a supervising teacher or a school administrator, or directly intervene if the situation requires.

Supervising students and giving first aid

Whether non-teaching staff can be required to supervise students or give first aid depends on their experience and skills, the specified duties of the job and the relevant industrial award or agreement. Any non-teaching staff unsure about this should seek legal advice or contact their union.

If non-teaching staff are in a supervisory role, for example, at an excursion or camp, they must carry out their supervision conscientiously.

If non-teaching staff are asked to carry out basic first aid for students who have minor injuries, or to 'keep an eye' on students in the sick bay, they are expected to exercise due care as employees when doing this. However, a duty of care still rests with the school, so if the school has asked a non-teaching staff member to administer first aid and that staff member is not competent to do this, the school might be in breach of its duty of care. Accordingly, it is the school that might incur legal liability for any injury that results, as it has not exercised due care in selecting or training staff to carry out this important task. It is therefore advisable for non-teaching staff to have first-aid training if they are to be given this role, and that clear protocols are in place.

It is the school's responsibility to ensure that they appoint appropriately skilled staff to jobs involving safety of equipment or premises, and that staff receive adequate training.

Duty of trainee teachers

Trainees could be held responsible where their careless supervision of students causes injuries, and might not be covered by the exemptions given to volunteers (see 'Volunteers', p. 35). However, liability will still fall primarily on the school.

Teacher's duty to supervise

If you are required to supervise non-teaching staff and trainees, you must do so carefully to ensure students' safety. This includes ensuring that instructions are clear and understood. You should not require trainees to do tasks beyond their level of skill or experience. Failure to supervise carefully can be a breach of the duty of care if it contributes to a student's injury.

CHECKLIST

- ☑ Do the terms of non-teaching staff's employment allow for supervising students or giving first aid?
- ☑ Are non-teaching staff safety conscious and adequately trained to do their jobs safely?
- ☑ Supervise non-teaching staff and trainee teachers carefully.
- ☑ Do not ask trainees to act beyond their level of competence.

VOLUNTEERS

Volunteers, usually parents, are used in many ways in schools—as helpers in the classroom, in the school canteen, with sports, camps and excursions.

Working With Children Check (WWCC)
In all states and territories, it is mandatory for those working with children in schools to undergo a screening test. However, there are differences across the jurisdictions as to the type of screening, records checked and exemptions.

Schools using volunteers should check with the relevant body in their state or territory. No volunteers should be used unless they have a current WWCC (or equivalent).

School's liability for students' injuries
When a volunteer supervises a student group, the school still owes a duty of care to those students (see 'Duty of care', p. 5). The school will probably be liable where students are injured as a result of the carelessness of a volunteer. Accordingly, schools should:
- ensure that the school's insurance policy or the department's indemnity policy covers liability for negligent acts of volunteers that cause personal injury or property damage to others
- avoid leaving volunteers in charge of groups unless it is absolutely necessary, and the volunteer is clearly competent to handle that particular group.

If volunteers use their own cars to transport students, the school should receive informed consent from the parents of the child to be transported. Also, the school has a duty to assess the driver's competence. For example, students should not travel with a driver who has been drinking.

Volunteer's liability for students' injuries

The law now protects volunteers from personal liability for injuries caused by their carelessness. However, this protection might not operate in any of the following circumstances:

- if the volunteer was drunk, under the influence of drugs, committing a crime, not acting in good faith or acting outside the authority given to them by the school
- when driving a motor vehicle, where the duty to students is the same as the duty to any other passenger in the car.

Volunteer's injuries

Teachers and other school staff are covered by a state or territory workers' compensation scheme for personal injuries they suffer in the course of their employment. Volunteers are not employees and should check on the extent of any school or education department insurance policies covering personal injuries and property damage suffered by volunteers in accidents. A volunteer could sue the school if their injury was caused by the school's carelessness or failure to provide safe premises.

Volunteers injured in a car accident are covered by the compulsory third-party personal injury insurance scheme operating in their state or territory.

CHECKLIST

- ☑ Does the volunteer have a current WWCC or equivalent?
- ☑ Does the school's insurance policy or the department's indemnity policy cover injuries or property damage caused by the careless acts of volunteers?
- ☑ Should you be leaving a volunteer in charge of a group?
- ☑ Does the volunteer realise that taking charge of a group involves accepting a duty of care for their safety?
- ☑ Is there insurance covering a volunteer for personal injuries suffered while volunteering?
- ☑ Will a volunteer be reimbursed for damage to their property?

FIRST AID AND DISEASE

This section should be read in conjunction with 'Duty of care' (p. 5).

The school should have policies and procedures for dealing with diseases, emergencies requiring first aid (including the use of an autoinjector) and blood spills. You should be familiar with the policies and procedures and know where a first-aid kit and gloves, etc. for blood spills are kept. If the school has not made such arrangements, you should bring it to the attention of the school, the occupational health and safety representative or your union.

Administering first aid

The duty of care requires you to take control of any health emergency that you come across, but it does not necessarily require you personally to administer first aid. You should be aware which members of staff have first-aid training. School administrations should inform teachers about students with conditions that can create emergencies (e.g. allergies, asthma, epilepsy) and procedures should be established for managing those individual students.

If you come across an accident and you don't have first-aid training, you should:
- send a student to get someone with training
- send for a doctor or ambulance to be called if the injury is serious
- carry out basic first aid if it looks like help will be some time in coming and a failure to render

assistance might have serious consequences (e.g. keep the student warm, stop the flow of blood).

You are not expected to exercise the skill of a doctor or a nurse—the duty of care will have been fulfilled if you have done what a reasonable person would do in that situation.

As soon as possible, write a detailed report on what happened, the procedures followed and the names of any witnesses. This report may become evidence if the incident ends up in court.

Contagious diseases

The school's duty of care to its students requires it to inform you if any student has a serious contagious disease (e.g. measles) and to request that the student stay at home during the period of contagion.

Infectious diseases and blood spills

The duty of care does not require you to expose yourself to the risk of infection. However, the duty does require you to protect your students from a known danger of infection. Accordingly, you should keep students away from others' blood and arrange to have spilled blood cleaned up safely.

A school must not discriminate against a student because they are carrying a disease-causing organism, such as HIV. However, where someone has a disease that can be transmitted at school, it is not discriminatory to treat that person differently in order to protect the health of students or staff (see 'Discrimination', p. 82).

Consideration should also be given to issues of confidentiality (see 'Confidential information from students', p. 95).

Administering medication

The duty of care does not require you to administer medication to students or to give injections, and you cannot be ordered to do this as you are not trained or employed for these tasks. Nevertheless, teachers and non-teaching staff, particularly at primary schools, are often asked by parents to administer medication. If you agree, you must obtain specific instructions from the parent. Once you have agreed to accept this responsibility, you are expected to exercise reasonable care when carrying it out. Staff who feel that they cannot accept that responsibility should not agree to it and other arrangements should be made for administering the medication. It is advisable for schools to develop a policy on medication to clarify this issue.

Students with health conditions that put them at risk

Principals of schools must take special care to comply with legal requirements in respect of students with known medical conditions such as anaphylaxis, diabetes, asthma, epilepsy or other conditions that could affect their health at school.

Additional attention also needs to be given to the duty of care and complying with legislation governing discrimination, bullying and health and safety.

All states and territories have legislation or guidelines in place, which schools must follow to discharge their duty of care to students with known medical conditions. This usually involves the development of an individual healthcare plan, which is communicated to the staff who will have responsibility for the student.

Anaphylaxis

It is the legal responsibility of the principal of the school, rather than individual teachers, to devise a specific management plan suited to the needs of a student who has been diagnosed as being at risk of anaphylaxis (which is a sudden, severe allergic reaction). All students at risk of anaphylaxis should have an Australasian Society of Clinical Immunology and Allergy (ASCIA) Action Plan for Anaphylaxis. All teaching staff should be familiar with the ASCIA plan and follow it in an emergency. If you become aware that a child is at risk of anaphylaxis, and no plan is in place, you should immediately bring the matter to the attention of the principal so that a plan can be devised. A management plan should be developed through consultation with the child's parents and medical practitioner.

The school must develop its own policy and procedures to manage students at risk of anaphylaxis. The policy should include training in emergency responses, including the administering of an adrenaline autoinjector (such as an EpiPen or Anapen), for all teaching staff and non-teaching staff who could be required to supervise the students at risk. This would include supervision on yard duty, school camps, and so on.

It is the school's responsibility to ensure the training takes place, and that there is a proper communication plan providing relevant information to staff and students. The frequency of training will vary from state to state but should be at least once a year. Victorian schools are required by legislation and *Ministerial Order No. 90* to have twice-yearly booster training. In New South Wales it is mandatory to comply with *Anaphylaxis Procedures for Schools 2012*.

Once you have received anaphylaxis emergency response training, you are not expected to have the knowledge and skills of a nurse or medical practitioner. Your duty of care requires you to exercise only the level of skill that could be reasonably expected of someone who has received that level of training. However, the level of training should equip you with the skill and confidence to administer the autoinjector (EpiPen/Anapen) in an emergency and call an ambulance.

In those states and territories where schools may have staff who have not yet been trained, a trained member of staff should be available on camps and excursions to remote areas. In all cases where a student diagnosed with anaphylaxis shows symptoms of an anaphylactic event, the autoinjector should be administered and an ambulance called. Where a staff member does not feel confident to administer the autoinjector they should follow the instructions of the ambulance officer on the phone.

Senior school students may take responsibility for carrying and administering their own autoinjector. However, younger children and senior school children who are unconscious will need assistance from a staff member.

Each student at risk of anaphylaxis should have a prescribed adrenaline autoinjector, together with the ASCIA Action Plan, stored in an accessible place. Schools should have at least one adrenaline autoinjector stored as a backup for general use. There should also be another backup for camps and excursions. School policy should include procedures for recording the expiry dates of the adrenaline autoinjectors (including those prescribed for individual students) and a system for checking when autoinjectors need to be replaced.

The importance of communicating medical information and of staff training cannot be overstressed. In a Victorian coronial inquiry into the death of a student on a college army cadet camp, the coroner held that the boy's death resulted from a failure of the school to exercise reasonable care and attention. Although the parents had provided the school with medical and food allergy information, the school had not adequately communicated this to the camp personnel. The boy had a severe anaphylactic reaction to the food in his ration pack, which was found to contain peanuts. A 10-minute delay by the staff in administering his EpiPen also contributed to the cause of death.[1]

Asthma

Asthma is a reasonably common condition in children. For each child diagnosed with asthma, the school should have in place:
- an action plan
- a student health support plan
- readily available asthma reliever medication.

All teachers and support staff should be informed of the student's needs and the location of the asthma action plan. The school should provide asthma information and training for all staff and provide the location of the asthma reliever. An asthma reliever should be included in all first-aid kits for excursions.

CHECKLIST

- ☑ Familiarise yourself with school policies and procedures for emergencies.
- ☑ Check which teachers have first-aid training.
- ☑ If you are not trained in first aid, only administer it if a trained person is not available.
- ☑ Protect yourself and your students from blood spills.
- ☑ You cannot be made to take responsibility for administering medication, but if you do, you should exercise care when carrying out that responsibility.
- ☑ Take detailed notes as soon as possible after an incident, including the names of witnesses, procedures followed and instructions given.
- ☑ If you become aware that a child is at risk of anaphylaxis, bring this to the attention of the principal so that an individual management plan can be devised for that student.
- ☑ Become familiar with your school policy and state/territory legislation/guidelines on anaphylaxis and asthma.

Continued...

- ☑ Make sure you know which students are at risk of anaphylaxis and/or asthma and are familiar with their action plans.
- ☑ Know where to locate an ASCIA Action Plan and adrenaline autoinjector (EpiPen/Anapen) for a student at risk of anaphylaxis in an emergency.
- ☑ Know where to locate asthma reliever medication.
- ☑ Make sure you know how to administer an autoinjector in an emergency, or, have quick access to someone who does.
- ☑ Make sure you have a backup autoinjector and asthma reliever medication for camps and excursions.

PANDEMICS

Student health has been threatened by three worldwide outbreaks of new respiratory virus strains in the past 20 years: SARS in 2003, H1N1 (swine flu) in 2009 and COVID-19 in 2020. All schools need a Critical Incidents Policy with procedures to protect the health and welfare of students and staff in the event of future pandemics and to maximise the capacity for recovery when the pandemic has subsided.

All members of the school will need to keep up to date with federal and state policies and pandemic planning.

Hygiene

It is the responsibility of the school to clean and disinfect common areas and to ensure that sufficient supplies of soap, paper towels, antiseptic wipes and sanitiser are available. The teachers and support staff have a duty to ensure that:
- their classrooms display up-to-date posters with information on good hygiene practices
- students follow those practices.

Quarantine and self-isolation

Students and staff may be required to remain in quarantine if they:
- are returning to Australia from overseas
- entering a state that has a required quarantine period
- have been in contact with a confirmed case of the illness

- show symptoms of the illness, until cleared.

You will need to develop teaching materials to cater for your students who are physically present and for those who are at home. Students required to stay at home should not be disadvantaged.

In the event that the school is ordered to close part or all of its campus, or, if the school is not able to function normally because of the number of staff and students at home you must be prepared to:
- work from home
- deliver courses online
- operate as part of a skeleton staff
- take part in online virtual meetings with colleagues and students
- keep parents up to date and fully informed
- ensure that all students are supported.

Under the Australian Constitution, responsibility for schooling lies with the states. In 2020, in response to the health risks posed by COVID-19, each state made its own decision on whether to close its schools based on the advice of its chief medical officer. The Catholic and Independent sectors were free to make their own decisions, bearing in mind that the bulk of their funding came from the federal government, and federal government advice in some cases was in conflict with state advice. Almost all teachers were at some point delivering online lessons coupled with onsite supervision for students who were not able to stay at home.

This was a difficult time for teachers. Teachers were required to plan their delivery of curriculum in a variety of settings and to adapt to changing policy as the health advice changed.

Online courses and the duty of care

Attendance and learning
The fact that students are at home does not absolve teachers of their duty of care. For the duration of the school day, students are effectively at school but working from a remote location. You are advised to:
- monitor attendance through a checklist provided by virtual classroom technology or regular check-in procedures
- hold classes during normal school hours
- inform students and parents of the online requirements and your expectations of students
- teach the curriculum using web-based tools suited to the technology and skills of students
- regularly assess student progress and give feedback
- provide opportunities for all students to learn.

Welfare and safety
Web-based learning frees the student and the teacher from the controls operating in a physical classroom setting. While it can extend the scope of the learning experience, it opens the student to dangers inherent in the technology. To protect students, you are advised to:
- only use communication channels and software approved by the school
- make regular contact with students to check on their welfare
- maintain your professional appearance and tone
- not be drawn into personal conversations
- establish clear expectations of students' online behaviour
- report to the school and make provision for a welfare check on students who fail to sign in to virtual classes or to check in on a regular basis

- resist being drawn into providing advice outside your learning areas
- refer any student in need of counselling to the appropriate professional services
- remember your legal obligations, including mandatory reporting (see p. 126)
- keep in mind when running virtual classrooms or group sessions that some students may feel vulnerable in their home environment.

Group sessions bring the classroom into the student's home, possibly exposing hurtful comparisons. To protect students from embarrassment or bullying:

- it is preferable that group sessions be conducted in anonymous settings by blurring backgrounds or changing background images. Software should be chosen that allows the student to do this and students should be trained to place themselves in an anonymous setting
- students should be instructed to present themselves at virtual classes in their school uniforms or in clean and neat clothes.

For the safety of both the student and the teacher and to avoid grooming or any accusations of grooming:

- you should not hold private one-on-one conferencing sessions with a student
- if there is a need for a one-on-one session, you should make sure that the student has a parent or another adult present; or
- you should have another teacher as witness to the conversation.

As a pandemic comes under control, the school moves to recovery mode. The students return to their classrooms. The teachers and the support staff now have a duty to keep the students safe in the classroom and to prevent the spread of disease. If social distancing is required, this can be achieved by:

- arranging classrooms so that students are spaced according to recommended state or federal health guidelines
- conducting outside lessons where possible
- staggering lesson and arrival times so that students don't all arrive and leave at the same time
- employing group work only in situations where social distancing can be achieved.

Hygiene will still be of the utmost importance, with classrooms being regularly cleaned, equipment disinfected and posters displaying required hygiene practices remaining in prominent positions.

CHECKLIST

- ☑ Familiarise yourself with your school's Critical Incidents Policy and pandemic action plans.
- ☑ Keep up to date with state and federal information and advice.
- ☑ Keep up to date with developments in communication technology and explore the most effective and safest online tools for the delivery of your curriculum.
- ☑ Do not use technology that is not approved or recommended by your school.
- ☑ Ensure that you have the technology and the skills to:
    - ☑ work at home
    - ☑ deliver your lessons and activities online
    - ☑ attend virtual meetings.
- ☑ Above all, be aware that your duty of care extends to the delivery of lessons online. As in the physical classroom, you must take reasonable care to protect your students from foreseeable harm and to deliver educational outcomes to a standard expected of a competent teacher.
- ☑ Remain flexible and arrange your classroom and teaching program to achieve social distancing as required.
- ☑ Vigilantly enforce safe hygiene practices.

PART 2

Discipline, physical contact and relations with students

STUDENT DISCIPLINE AND RESTRAINT

Teachers today have more responsibility and accountability for their charges than their counterparts a hundred years ago. At the same time, they are more restricted in the methods of discipline they can use.

Government schools

The power of government schools and their teachers to discipline students comes from education department regulations and policies. On the basis of these, schools develop their own rules and practices. When you are new to a school you should familiarise yourself with the school's discipline policies and procedures. A certain punishment may be lawful, but unacceptable to a particular school's policy and lead to disciplinary action against you.

Non-government schools

In non-government schools, parents enter into a contractual relationship with the school to educate the child, and this involves agreeing to the school's discipline rules. Parents can object to a particular discipline practice (e.g. Saturday detentions), and if the school accepts the objection, teachers will not have the power to use that discipline technique.

Corporal punishment

Corporal punishment is not allowed in any government schools. It is not allowed in most non-government schools either because of government regulation (ACT, NSW, SA, Tas, Vic, WA) or by school policy.

Queensland is the only state that has not prohibited the use of corporal punishment in non-government schools. However, both the Catholic and independent schools have stated that they have no intention of using corporal punishment.

Scope of your powers

You can exercise a traditional range of disciplinary powers to ensure that you maintain good order while students are in your care, provided they do not involve ridicule and humiliation (discussed below), and bearing in mind the restrictions on corporal punishment.

Traditional discipline methods are not, however, inherent powers that a teacher has. If a school's discipline policy instructs you not to exercise any particular discipline methods, then you no longer have that particular power. While it is lawful to detain a student for a short while at the end of class for a private conversation, any longer period should only be in accordance with government regulation and the school's policy on detentions.

Due to the school's duty of care to adequately supervise students, if a student is 'sent from the room', it should only be to report to a supervised place, and in accordance with an established school policy (see 'Duty of care', p. 5). The matter should be followed up at the end of class.

A punishment that causes physical discomfort (e.g. making a child stand for a long period of time) could amount to corporal punishment.

Discrimination

Punishments should not differentiate, directly or indirectly, on the basis of sex, gender identity, race or ethnicity (see 'Discrimination', including the definition of indirect discrimination, p. 82).

Ridicule and humiliation

While teachers can chastise students, you should avoid using discipline methods that involve ridicule and humiliation that could amount to bullying. Such discipline could contravene the United Nations Convention on the Rights of the Child and, if it amounts to extreme and prolonged bullying or humiliation, could lead to the child suing the school for compensation for profound emotional damage. Not only must you ensure that your conduct could not be construed as discriminatory, harassing or bullying, you have a duty to intervene to protect students from such harmful behaviour from other students (see 'Bullying, harassment and assault', p. 72)

Comments that contravene anti-discrimination laws (such as those that are sexist, racist, or about a person's physical features, disability, religious or political beliefs, or sexual preference) should be avoided (see 'Discrimination', p. 82).

Restraint

You can use as much force as is necessary to prevent students from injuring themselves or others, or to stop a dangerous situation from developing. Hence it is lawful for you to physically break up fights, or to restrain a student who is about to assault someone or damage property. However, it would be reasonable for you not to intervene in a fight where to do so could lead to injury to you or a student. In its review of *Moran v Victorian Institute of Teachers*, the Victorian Civil and Administrative Tribunal (VCAT) overturned a decision of the Victorian Institute of Teachers to deregister the teacher, in favour of suspension. In coming to this decision the VCAT panel made the following statement:

> *In our view, there is no immutable rule that a teacher should physically intervene in a fight between students.*

There are many occasions when it would be physically dangerous to the teacher, or to one of the students, to do so. A teacher is not required to risk his physical safety, or that of another student in the discharge of his professional responsibility.[1]

The panel recognised that there would be occasions when it would be safe for a teacher to intervene but this must be a judgment call on the teacher's part.

The use of excessive force—that is, going beyond prevention of the danger and actually punishing the student— could amount to an assault (see 'Physical contact and sexual assault', p. 65). Excessive force is not easy to define, and will depend on all the circumstances. For example, threatening a fleeing student with a heavy object is likely to be more force than is necessary. On the other hand, if a teacher fails to try to stop a student behaving dangerously and someone is injured, the teacher's duty of care may not have been met (see 'Duty of care', p. 5). You should not put yourself in danger—if a potentially dangerous situation arises, send for help and use voice control to try and maintain order.

In Victoria, Regulation 25 of the *Education and Training Reform Regulations 2017* provides that:

A member of staff of a Government school may take any reasonable action that is immediately required to restrain a student of the school from acts or behaviour that is dangerous to the member of staff, the student, or any other person.[2]

Where restraint is reasonable, you should use the minimum force necessary to avoid the danger, taking into account the age, size and known disabilities of the student. Mechanical restraints should never be used. If your school has a policy on restraint, make sure you stay within the school guidelines. Do not hold the student so as to restrict breathing. Do not force the student to the ground. You should always take care in how you restrain a student, to avoid allegations of sexual assault. The Victorian Department of Education has some guidelines at https://www2.education.vic.gov.au/pal/restraint-seclusion/resources.

In the case of any incident involving restraint, you should inform your principal and make detailed notes of the incident.

If a student insists on leaving a class or school activity without permission, they should not be physically restrained unless they are endangering themselves or others. Send someone to report it to the principal or other senior teacher, and follow it up after class. The police should be notified if it is appropriate. It may be necessary to restrain very young children, as it would be dangerous to let them run away.

If it is known that a student is prone to violent behaviour, any staff members who could be at risk of injury from the student should be given this information. Disclosing this sort of information does not breach privacy laws where the information is necessary to reduce a serious risk to health.

A violent student may be restrained until the police or the student's parents arrive. The force used must be in proportion to the danger, and the student should be handed over to the police or the parents as soon as practicable.

Health and safety laws (WHS/OHS/OSH) require employers to provide a safe place of work. Accordingly, the school administration must address the safety problems that arise where a student is known to be violent. Furthermore, under the safely laws, an employee has a duty to care for his own safety as well as that of others in the workplace.

In summary:
- physical restraint of students should only be used as a last resort when all non-physical interventions have been exhausted

- use only minimum force. Excessive use of force may result in allegations of child abuse[3], a civil suit[4] or even a criminal charge, as has happened in the United States[5]
- physical restraint should only be used where there is immediate risk of injury to another person, or, an immediate risk of property damage
- physical restraint should not be used if there is a risk of injury to a staff member
- mechanical restraints should never be used.

Searches

Teachers do not have the power to search students, and it is unwise to attempt to do so (see 'Physical contact and sexual assault', p. 65). You can, however, ask students to reveal what is in their pockets if you reasonably believe they are carrying something dangerous. If a personal search is thought to be necessary because the student might be carrying an item that could endanger staff or students, the police should be called. The duty of care requires effective action to be taken where there is a reasonably foreseeable risk of injury.

You can search a student's bag, provided that the student does not object to the search. If it is a school rule that bags can be searched by staff, then the student cannot object to the search; however, physical force should not be used if the student resists the search. In those circumstances, if it is thought that a search of the bag is important (e.g. because it contains drugs, a weapon or stolen goods), the police should be called.

Lockers are usually the property of the school, and consequently may be searched without the student's permission.

Mobile phones

Schools need to develop clear policies on the use of mobile phones. While mobile phones have some educational value, the school may assess the unregulated use of the phone as a distraction and as disruptive to learning. The policies differ from state to state and from school to school. Teachers need to familiarise themselves with their school policy. In Victoria, for example, from Term 1 2020, students in government schools who choose to bring mobile phones to school must have them switched off and securely stored during school hours. Use of the mobile phone during school hours may be authorised by a teacher under one of the listed exemptions.

Mobile phones are the property of the student (or possibly their parents). Seizure and search of the phone without reasonable justification could give rise to an action in trespass and could be a breach of privacy.

If the school rules permit you to confiscate a student's phone, you may do so provided you stay within the limits set out in the rules (i.e. the student is using the phone in a manner forbidden by the school rules). The phone must be returned to the student at the very latest by the end of the day.

If a student refuses to hand over a phone you should not attempt to take it by force, but report the student's refusal to the school management and rely upon the school's disciplinary procedures.

The teacher's right to search a student's phone without the student's permission is a grey area and most of the case law comes from the United States. Unless the student has given consent to the search, you should only proceed with a search of a phone with extreme caution and preferably after having received legal advice. However, you have a duty of care to keep all students safe and to protect the learning environment. A search of a student's mobile phone could be justified if you have reasonable cause to believe that the

phone is being used in harmful activities, for example that the student is:
- using the phone to breach school rules (e.g. cheating in an examination)
- putting other students at risk (e.g. by texting threatening or bullying messages)
- at risk themselves (e.g. of suicide)
- involved in sexting with other students and/or distributing explicit images
- in an inappropriate relationship with a staff member.

In these circumstances, a limited search of the phone could be justified, but you must limit the search to matters that gave rise to the reasonable suspicion of harmful activity. For example, if you had a reasonable suspicion that a student was receiving texts so that they could cheat in an examination, it could be permissible to search the immediate text messages on the phone, but it would be a breach of the student's rights to search or copy the contents, or, to go on a fishing expedition (an open-ended investigation not based on solid evidence, undertaken in the hope of uncovering embarrassing or damaging information). In a 2010 case from the United States, a 17-year-old student received damages in the order of $33 000 for the invasion of her rights when the principal of her high school searched her confiscated phone and found semi-nude pictures of the girl herself. The pictures had been taken by the internal camera of the phone and had never been circulated, but the principal handed them to the law enforcement agency and gave the girl a three-day suspension from school.[6] There have been similar cases in the United States that have settled with the student receiving damages.

A further word of warning: if you or any other staff member does come across a compromising or unlawful photograph on a student device, you should not copy it onto your own device as evidence, lest your motive is misinterpreted and you are charged with possessing child pornography.

Sexting

With the increased use of mobile phones by children and young people, the practice of sexting (using a mobile phone camera to take and send nude or semi-nude photographs to other mobile phones or internet sites) is becoming more prevalent. Recent surveys show that over 20% of teenagers have participated in sexting.[7] Interviews with groups of students demonstrate that they have little awareness of the law and the penalties they risk.[8]

Current federal legislation dictates that children who engage in sexting are regarded as participating in child pornography; students who exchange nude or semi-nude photographs may be accused of possessing, making and distributing pornographic images even though the exchange was consensual. Charges may be brought, and there's a possibility of placement on the Sex Offenders' Register. While state laws differ, federal law classifies sexting behaviour by young people under the age of 18 as participating in child pornography under the *Criminal Code Act 1995*. Where there is a clash between state law and federal law, the state attorney general may need to be consulted before federal charges proceed.

Under recent changes to the law in Victoria[9] and New South Wales[10], children under the age of 18 who sext one another will no longer be guilty of child pornography, provided both parties consented. Similarly, Western Australia no longer regards the distribution of self-images by consenting young persons (over the age of 16) as a criminal offence. Where a young person appears to have committed an offence the police will have discretion to issue a caution instead of proceeding to a criminal charge.[11]

The Victorian parliament recently amended the *Sex Offenders Registration Act 2004* (Vic) to give judges discretion to exempt an 18- or 19-year-old offender from automatic registration as a sex offender. New South Wales has now provided courts with limited discretion when deciding whether to register a person who was under 18 when the offence was committed. For some time, Tasmania has allowed judicial discretion in the registration of adult sex offenders.

However, while some states have relaxed their pursuit of young people engaged in consensual exchange of images, the laws in other areas have been tightened and there are stiff penalties where consent is lacking. Schools may still be faced with the consequences of non-consensual distribution of such illegal images. In addition, the school may have to deal with issues of sexual harassment, cyberbullying and child abuse (see 'Cyberbullying', p. 75).

What can schools do to protect the school and students from the risks posed by sexting?

Schools have a duty of care to their students and should take action, in so far as it is under their control to do so, to protect their students from the potential harms of sexting. Some actions that schools can take are listed below:

- Inform students that by participating in sexting they may be in breach of the child pornography laws.
- Make students aware of the penalties and the consequences of being listed on the Sex Offenders' Register.
- Warn students that they can easily lose control of images sent to a digital device and, if posted on the internet (which may happen without their consent), they may never be able to delete them.
- Invite local police officers to talk to students about the harm and legal ramifications of sexting.
- Expressly prohibit sexting under the school rules and apply clear penalties to those who breach the rules.
- Put in place monitoring procedures.

- Immediately delete any nude or sexual images found on the school network and, if traceable, commence disciplinary procedures.

Schools should also have a comprehensive 'Acceptable Use of Technology' agreement in place that sets out the ethical and behaviour guidelines to which students must adhere if they use the school's network or their own devices while at school.

- Students should not be allowed to use the network until they have signed the agreement.
- As part of the agreement, students must accept that they will be identified by their username and password and that all communication (both internal and external) may be monitored by the school.

As mentioned earlier, if you have reason to believe that a student is distributing explicit sexual images on a mobile phone, you may be justified (in satisfying your duty of care) in conducting a search of the phone for the express purpose of locating the unlawful images.

Drug testing

In government schools, drug testing should only be carried out where it has been authorised by the government education authority, and in accordance with strict, authorised guidelines with regard to privacy and maintenance of dignity.

In non-government schools, parents can agree to the carrying out of random drug testing, in which case it becomes a term of the contract between parents and school. However, careful guidelines should be observed in relation to maintaining privacy and dignity in the carrying out of tests. Where a student objects to providing, for example, a urine test, force should not be used, as this will amount to an assault. While parents can agree to a drug-testing rule, they cannot give consent for their child to be assaulted.

Confiscations

You may confiscate items that disrupt classes, or are dangerous or forbidden by school rules. Confiscated items remain the property of students and the security of those items becomes your responsibility. Items that are lawful should be returned to the students or their parents, undamaged, at the end of the school day. Unlawful items (e.g. powerful laser pointers, knuckledusters, butterfly knives) should be given to the police.

Confiscation of prohibited substances

If you confiscate a prohibited drug from a student, you must hand it over as soon as possible to the police. If you do not do so, you open yourself up to a charge of possessing a prohibited substance.

CHECKLIST

- ☑ Know the school discipline policy and ensure that your discipline methods are consistent with it.
- ☑ Avoid differentiating on the basis of sex, gender, sexual orientation or race when administering discipline.
- ☑ Avoid ridicule and humiliation when disciplining students.
- ☑ Reasonable force can be used to restrain students who endanger themselves or others. If restraint is used, immediately inform your principal. Make detailed contemporaneous notes of the incident.
- ☑ While you should take effective action to deal with violent student behaviour, you are not required to put yourself in danger.
- ☑ Do not carry out personal searches of students.
- ☑ Only confiscate student private items if the school rules allow or the school has reasonable justification (i.e. reasonable suspicion of unlawful activity or danger to students).

Continued...

- ☑ Do not conduct a search of a student's mobile phone unless you have the student's consent to do so, or have reasonable justification. Limit the search to the area that gave rise to the reasonable suspicion of unlawful activity or breach of school rules.
- ☑ The school should review its policies and ensure that it has clear rules and disciplinary procedures covering the use of mobile phones and other devices.
- ☑ Make students aware that sexting could involve them in a criminal offence. Even if changes to state laws may have decriminalised sexting between consenting minors, the protections provided are limited and charges could still be laid under the federal *Criminal Code Act 1995* (Cth) legislation.

PHYSICAL CONTACT AND SEXUAL ASSAULT

For advice on the power of teachers to restrain students who are acting dangerously, see 'Student discipline and restraint', p. 52.

Touching students

Encouraging pats on the shoulder or arm are a normal part of everyday interaction between people, not just in schools, and it is common, and not against the law, for teachers to comfort emotionally distressed students by touching in a supportive way.

Touching of a non-sexual nature will only amount to an assault if the student has not consented to it. A Queensland Court of Appeal case suggested that students tacitly consent to receiving tactile encouragement (such as a pat on the shoulder), and that not allowing this would make schools sterile places. But, the court added, children do not consent to prolonged or effusive physical contact. Furthermore, children can withdraw their consent, either by word or gesture.[1]

Unless a school has adopted a policy of never touching students except in emergencies, moderate encouraging, congratulatory and supportive touching of students by teachers is permissible. However, you must be sensitive to whether this causes students any discomfort, and must stop if it does. Also, you should always bear in mind that, while your intention might be to encourage or support a student, the student might interpret the touching as 'sleazy' or sexual. For this reason, many teachers adopt a policy of never touching students, or avoid placing themselves in a situation (e.g. alone in a concealed area) where an allegation of sexual impropriety might be difficult to refute.

Where touching clearly has a sexual quality to it (e.g. touching breasts or the genital area) a teacher can be charged with indecent assault (see 'Sexual harassment', p. 92).

Sexual contact with students

It is a serious crime for a teacher (male or female) to have sexual intercourse with a student from their school. This applies to students under 16 years of age in the Australian Capital Territory and Queensland; under 17 in Tasmania or under 18 in New South Wales, South Australia, Victoria, Western Australia and Northern Territory; even if the student has consented. The remaining states and the ACT are under pressure to adopt 18 as the age at which sexual acts between a teacher and a student become lawful.[2] In addition to the age limits, the Victorian Institute of Teaching recently updated its code of conduct to restrict any sexualised relationship between a teacher and a student for two years after the student has competed their final year of secondary school.

A conviction for sexual contact with a student can lead to the teacher being deregistered and being placed on a child sex offender register. In some states there might be a defence where a teacher had reasonable grounds for believing a student had reached the age of consent, but given that teachers have access to records about students' ages, this would be difficult to prove.

The definition of sexual intercourse in most states is very wide, and can include intimate acts other than penetration. In addition, less intimate consensual sexual contact

Physical contact and sexual assault

can be an offence. Accordingly, you should avoid any sort of sexual contact with students.

A sexual relationship with a student is an extremely serious matter even if the relationship is consensual. Not only may the teacher be found unfit to teach, but a breach of the criminal law can also result in a prison sentence. In addition, the student may sue for damages for the emotional and psychological injury suffered as a consequence of the relationship.

Although schools have a non-delegable duty of care and will usually be held vicariously liable for the negligent (or unlawful) acts of their employees done in the course of their employment, schools will not be vicariously liable if a teacher has acted outside the scope of their employment and the school did not know of the relationship or could not have foreseen the teacher's wrongful actions.

In a recent case in New South Wales, a female teacher who was 29 at the start of the relationship was found to have commenced a sexual relationship with one of her students who turned 18 shortly after the relationship began. The boy had learning difficulties and behavioural problems and attended a special school where the teacher taught. Knowing his vulnerability, the teacher should have fulfilled her duty of care to a high standard. The boy sued both the state and the teacher for emotional and psychological problems that resulted from the relationship. The trial judge found the teacher liable and the state vicariously liable and awarded damages.[3]

On appeal, the employer—the State of New South Wales—was found not vicariously liable, as there was insufficient nexus between the employment and the unauthorised act. The appeal court held the teacher had acted independently. The student was able to recover damages from the teacher but not from the state.[4]

You are reminded that sexting is a criminal offence that could see you convicted of the possession of child pornography and listed on the Sex Offenders' Register, which would make it impossible to work with children in the future.

Where an incident has occurred or an allegation has been made, make careful, detailed notes as soon as possible and seek advice from your lawyer or union. Notes should be kept as part of official school records, rather than as your personal property.

Grooming a child under 16

Grooming involves befriending a child and/or the child's parents and/or carers with the intention of having a sexual relationship with the child at some future date.

Legislation in New South Wales and Victoria[5] makes it an offence to groom a child under 16 for the purposes of making it easier to procure the child for unlawful sexual activity. Grooming usually involves an adult gaining the trust of a vulnerable child over a period of time by giving them extra attention, friendship and affection in order to draw the child into a secretive relationship for the purpose of sexual contact. It may involve providing a child with an intoxicating substance, or engaging in conduct that exposes them to indecent material.

In South Australia, it is also a criminal offence to communicate for a prurient purpose and with the intention of making a child amenable to sexual activity.

All states and territories have legislation making online grooming an offence.

Inappropriate relationships

Teachers should also take care not to become involved in improper relationships with students, as such relationships can threaten the teacher's employment, and could lead to cancellation or suspension of a teacher's registration.

These are relationships that while not involving any sexual contact, are characterised by very close emotional ties, and sometimes involve expressions of love or deep affection. Such relationships can be seen as unprofessional and crossing the professional boundaries marking the appropriate distance between teacher and student. Young teachers who are close in age to their students are particularly vulnerable here, and older teachers can help young teachers avoid the problem through appropriate counselling, or by recommending professional counselling. Cases that have gone before teacher discipline hearings have often involved intimate texting and emailing between teacher and student.

Teachers must take care to maintain appropriate boundaries in the teacher–student relationship. You may find yourself compromised if you involve yourself in telephone conversations, text messages or electronic correspondence without a valid educational context.

Similarly, you should think twice before:
- attending a student's private party (unless invited by the parents who will be there as hosts)
- taking a student for a coffee or social event
- inviting a student to your home (particularly if there will be no one else present)
- giving money or gifts to students
- accepting gifts from students (other than small end-of-year thank-you gifts)
- becoming involved in discussions of students' personal lives.

A recent Victorian case illustrates the dangers for a teacher who oversteps the boundaries of appropriate conduct. Although the teacher was acquitted by a jury of a grooming offence, his career as a teacher was over.[6]

You must be aware of and comply with the guidelines, protocols or policies provided by your employer.

Social networking

There is an ongoing debate on whether teachers should or should not have students as 'friends' on Facebook or other social networking sites. Problems can arise if the boundaries between the professional life and the personal life of the teacher become blurred. For this reason, many employers (education departments and private schools) have decided to ban their employees from accepting students as friends on social media or social networking sites.

In 2012, Fair Work Australia considered an appeal by a teacher who had been disciplined for having students from her former school as friends on Facebook. The Fair Work Australia Commissioner dismissed the appeal, finding that the applicant had knowingly invited or accepted students as friends and that she had done so knowing that this activity was banned under her employer's code of practice.

If you do decide to accept students as friends, you should ensure that you are not contravening any regulations or codes that ban such activity. You should ensure that you are always in a professional relationship with your students whether at school or not. This would mean ensuring that:
- there is an educational context within which the site operates
- privacy settings are scrupulously set so that students are separated from your personal family and friends
- the site is carefully monitored to remove any inappropriate comments and access is denied to anyone who does not respect the rules.

CHECKLIST

- ☑ Check if your school has a policy on touching students. Follow the policy.
- ☑ Touching of students is permissible unless it is excessive or the student indicates verbally or by gesture that it is not welcome.
- ☑ Sexual touching of a student, or sexual relations with a student, are likely to be criminal offences and can lead to teacher deregistration.
- ☑ Take steps to avoid allegations, but if they have been made, seek advice before responding.
- ☑ Avoid developing intense emotional relationships with students, which could be regarded as 'improper' or unprofessional.
- ☑ It is advisable not to have student 'friends' on Facebook or other social networking sites.

BULLYING, HARASSMENT AND ASSAULT

Bullying and harassment are issues in most schools. As well as causing harm, they create potential legal problems for school administrators. Schools have a responsibility to deal with bullying and harassment and should have a policy setting out when and how to intervene.

What is bullying?

Bullying is when a person or a group repeatedly and intentionally use or abuse their power to intimidate, hurt, oppress or damage another person or group. Harassment occurs when a person is subjected to unwelcome, uninvited behaviour that they find offensive, humiliating, embarrassing or intimidating. Harassment can occur on any of the grounds of discrimination (e.g. display of offensive material or derogatory comments based on a person's race, colour sex, gender identity, sexual orientation, disability).

Bullying and harassment can be:
- physical, e.g. pushing, poking, tripping designed to hurt or humiliate
- verbal, e.g. name calling, insults, homophobic or racist slurs
- social, e.g. spreading lies, rumours, deliberate exclusion or playing nasty pranks
- psychological, e.g. intimidation, manipulation or stalking

- cyberbullying, e.g. the use of electronic devices to carry out verbal, social or psychological bullying.

What is not bullying?

Not every dispute is bullying. The following should not be treated as bullying:
- mutual quarrels or disagreements (where there is no power imbalance)
- single acts of nastiness, spite or social rejection
- random acts of anger
- legitimate conversations a principal or supervisor might have with a staff member about performance.

Legal remedies

Bullying can lead to legal action. Students who physically assault other students or teachers can be prosecuted for assault, or sued in a civil action for damages. You should report serious assaults to the police.

Continued harassment of a student by other students can amount to stalking. This can include harassment by email, text message and posting on social networking sites (cyberbullying), and the victim can apply for a court order against the stalkers. Cyberbullying and stalking, which have the intention of creating fear, may also be criminal offences, and the police should be contacted.

Abuse or harassment of a racial or sexual nature will contravene anti-discrimination laws.

Where a school fails to stop bullying about which it knew, or ought to have known, it could be a breach of the duty of care. A student who suffers physical or emotional injuries could sue the school for compensation.

This is an increasingly important issue for both government and private schools in Australia. In 2009, the Supreme Court of New South Wales awarded almost $470 000 in damages to a victim of bullying. The court accepted that the school was in breach of its duty of care and that the teachers had not responded to the victim's complaints or intervened to protect him.[1] Similarly, in 2010, a Victorian secondary student was awarded $290 000 in compensation over bullying incidents.[2]

Bullying and harassment policies

Schools should implement bullying and harassment policies, both to protect students and teachers, and to fulfil the school's legal liability. Policies should specify the sorts of behaviour that are unacceptable, and provide a clear set of grievance procedures for students who believe they are victims of harassment and/or bullying. Many school policies incorporate preventive strategies to encourage positive social behaviour.

Schools should have in place a system of supervision that gives adequate control over the students and provides reasonable protection for students against bullying. In addition, schools must have procedures that adequately deal with the mistreatment of a student by other students. In a recent case, the New South Wales Court of Appeal upheld an award of substantial damages to a student found to have been the subject of ongoing bullying.[3] While the school was not required to guarantee that the student would not be bullied, it did have a duty to take reasonable steps to ensure that the student was protected from bullying. Although the school did have a bullying policy and procedures, these were not put into effective practical operation. The court found that 'The steps which should have been taken by the College included keeping appropriate records; investigating the appellant's complaints; and dealing with both the perpetrator and the victim'.[4]

When following up a report of a bullying incident, you should not only follow the school's policy and procedures but should take notes detailing the incident and the action taken. Serious bullying is a criminal offence.

All Australian jurisdictions have stalking legislation proscribing behaviour calculated to harass, threaten or intimidate. Recent changes to the *Victorian Crimes Act* in 2011 mean that serious bullying is now classified in Victoria under the criminal offence of stalking. In theory, bullying at school, at work or online is punishable by a maximum term of 10 years' imprisonment. The change in law is known as Brodie's Law, after Brodie Panlock, who committed suicide having been subjected to horrific bullying in the workplace. Although the change in legislation arose from workplace bullying, it applies to all bullying situations, including those that arise in schools. The age of criminal responsibility is 10 years (with those between 10 and 14 only held liable if they knew that what they were doing was wrong). While the criminal law may seem too severe an approach to school bullying, student bullies should be warned that bullying is unlawful and severe consequences may follow if they do not stop.

Cyberbullying

The laws with respect to bullying also apply to cyberbullying, which has developed to be a serious problem in schools and in society in general. It has many similarities with offline bullying but it differs in that the bullies can be anonymous, it can reach a wide audience, it can operate 24/7 and the sent or uploaded material can be difficult to remove. Cyberbullying may be regarded as 'repeated' if the offensive material appears on Facebook, or other social networking sites, where it may be seen by many more people than the intended victim.

As with all serious bullying, cyberbullying is illegal and can be prosecuted under state and federal anti-stalking laws. It is an offence to use telecommunication services to menace, harass or cause offence, punishable by 3 years in prison. A threat to cause serious harm is punishable by 7 years and a threat to kill by 10 years.

Where a school becomes aware that other students are subjecting a student to cyberbullying, action should be taken, even if the students are sending or posting the offensive material out of school hours. The issue here is knowledge: did the school know, or, should it have known that the student was being mistreated? Although the school cannot control the home environment, the school does have control over the school environment and can implement disciplinary procedures against bullying perpetrators enrolled at the school. If the perpetrators are unknown, the school still has a duty of care to its student being bullied and should take reasonable action to report and prevent the mistreatment. Schools should have an 'Acceptable use of technology' agreement in place for all students (see 'Sexting', p. 60).

There is much information available in education literature on strategies for dealing with bullying. The National Safe Schools Framework and its resources, which deal with bullying, are available online (see 'Directory', p. 161).

Anti-discrimination agencies (see 'Directory', p. 159) can give advice on harassment policies (see 'Discrimination', p. 82).

Keeping students safe in a digitised world

Digital technologies are opening up new ways of teaching. The move to online learning during the COVID-19 lockdown intensified the move to use online instruction. Students are increasingly armed with portable devices whether supplied by the school, or, under a Bring Your Own Device school policy. These devices can be used outside of the traditional classroom, blurring the boundaries between school and home. It is clear that the school's duty of care extends beyond the physical boundaries of the school and beyond school hours (see 'Before and after school, p. 10). You must ask, 'Is there foreseeable risk to the student in using this technology or undertaking this activity?'. For example, a research activity that is safe when conducted in class may inadvertently expose the student to inappropriate adult content if the student uses the internet at home. If there is a foreseeable risk, then there is a duty to take reasonable precautions to eliminate or mitigate the risk.

Foreseeable internet risks include exposure of children to inappropriate adult content, cyberbullying (p. 75), harassment (p. 93), sexting (p. 60), grooming and sexual abuse (68), identity theft and loss of privacy. The greater the control the teacher has over the use of the online environment, the greater the duty. To increase control and minimise the risk, the school should have in place:
- acceptable use of technology agreements signed by the student and the student's parents
- capacity to monitor the online learning environment, including interactions between students and between students and teachers
- a system that encourages students to report any interaction that has made them feel uncomfortable or concerned
- a regular check-in with parents.

The duty of care does not extend to a realm outside the knowledge and control of the school or the teacher. However, where you know or should have known that a student was involved in risky or damaging interactions, you or the school may be held liable if you fail to act to protect the student.

Harassment of teachers

Teachers are sometimes threatened, stalked (including by email, text message or cyberbullying) or abused by students, parents or other members of the public. If a parent is difficult, you should inform the principal. Ideally, the school's welfare service should manage difficult, but non-threatening, conflicts between teachers and parents or students. However, it may be helpful to discuss these matters with your union or a lawyer. Schools, like all employers, are under an obligation to provide a safe workplace for their staff and should have policies and procedures in place to protect their workers. Serious matters should be reported to the police.

Criminal and civil legal proceedings can be brought against someone who threatens or assaults a teacher (see 'Trespass on school property', p. 146) and a court order obtained to prevent the behaviour from continuing. Teachers, like anyone, can use reasonable force to defend themselves if they are physically assaulted.

CHECKLIST

- ☑ Schools should have an anti-bullying policy and procedures, which you should follow.
- ☑ Schools should have an acceptable use of technology agreement, signed by both the students and parents.
- ☑ Systems should be developed to protect the student in an online environment.
- ☑ Schools can be in breach of their duty of care if they do not attempt to stop bullying.
- ☑ Always follow up a bullying complaint.
- ☑ Always follow school procedures and document the complaint and the action taken.
- ☑ There are legal remedies available for teachers or students who are victims of bullying.

PART 3

Provision of educational services

DISCRIMINATION

This section focuses on discrimination involving students. If you feel you have been discriminated against in employment as a teacher, you can obtain advice from your state or territory anti-discrimination agency (or the Australian Human Rights Commission), a union or a solicitor (see 'Directory', p. 159). Anti-discrimination law is covered by federal, state and territory legislation. Federal legislation applies to all Australians, whereas state or territory legislation applies only in the state or territory where it was enacted. In many cases federal and state laws overlap. However, there are differences between jurisdictions. Where state or territory law conflicts with federal law, the law of the Commonwealth prevails.

Grounds of discrimination

It is unlawful in all states and territories for an educational authority to discriminate against students because of any of the attributes identified in Commonwealth, state or territory legislation. The specifics of the federal legislation are listed below, and Table 3.1 (p. 86) lists the state and territory attributes. There is a large degree of overlap between the jurisdictions; however, where both state/territory and Commonwealth have legislated, one jurisdiction may provide a wider area of coverage than the other. Furthermore, some states have extended their anti-discrimination law into categories not covered by the Commonwealth or other jurisdictions. For example, only the Northern Territory and Tasmania have provided protection against discrimination on the basis of irrelevant medical records, and Victoria is the only state where it is unlawful to discriminate on the grounds of physical features (not including tattoos or body piercing).

Federal legislation protects against discrimination on the following grounds:
- race (includes skin colour, ancestry, national origin and ethnicity)
- sex
- sexual orientation (covers sexual orientation to persons of the same sex, different sex or both)
- gender identity (the way a person expresses their gender identity—includes transgender and gender diverse people)
- intersex status (covers features that are neither wholly male nor wholly female, a combination of female and male, or neither male nor female)
- marital or relationship status
- pregnancy and potential pregnancy
- breastfeeding
- family responsibility
- disability
  - total/partial loss of body or mental functions, disorder or malfunction that causes a person to learn differently, presence of organisms capable of causing disease/illness, malformation or disfigurement, mental illness
  - people with disability in possession of palliative/therapeutic devices/auxiliary aids
  - people with disability accompanied by an interpreter, reader, assistant or carer
  - people with disability accompanied by a guide dog or assistance animal
- age (exemption for some educational institutions established for particular age groups).

In addition, it is unlawful in some states and territories to discriminate because of the following attributes (although in New South Wales and Queensland these provisions only apply to government schools):
- religious or political belief or activity (all states and territories except New South Wales and South Australia. It is unlawful in South Australia to discriminate against religious appearance or dress in work or study)
- sexual orientation/activity (all states and territories)
- parental status (all states and territories).

The law in this area is complex and frequently changes as protected attributes are added by federal or state legislation. If in doubt seek legal advice.

Exemptions for schools

Schools may be exempt from some aspects of the anti-discrimination legislation.
- There is an exception for age, where an educational institution is established for people of particular ages.
- Non-government schools are exempted from some aspects of the state anti-discrimination legislation in New South Wales and Queensland.
- It is lawful to establish schools wholly for one sex, for one racial group (e.g. First Nations people), for a particular impairment (e.g. deaf students) or for a particular religious faith or age group.
- Coeducational schools in Victoria have successfully applied to the Victorian Civil and Administrative Tribunal for a temporary exemption from the *Equal Opportunity Act 2010* to allow them to advertise for students of a particular gender, in order to achieve a more equal balance between the number of boys and girls enrolled.
- Schools established by a particular religion can currently discriminate where it is necessary to avoid

offending their genuine religious beliefs. Under this exception, a religious school might regard it as lawful to discriminate against a student, or staff member, because of a lifestyle factor, or sexual orientation, where it is contrary to the school's religious teachings. However, the scope of this exception has not yet been tested fully by the courts, and the few cases that have been decided have interpreted the exception very narrowly, and often against the religious body's interests. Anyone who feels they might have been unfairly treated because the school believes their behaviour is contrary to religious belief should consult their lawyer or union.

The exemption provisions in the *Sex Discrimination Act 1984* that allow religious schools to exclude staff and students whose lifestyle (e.g. sexual orientation or gender identity) conflict with the school's religious beliefs and teaching are facing opposition. In 2018, the *Discrimination Free Schools Bill 2018*, introduced into federal parliament, sought the removal of anti-discrimination exceptions for religious schools. This bill did not become law. However, the whole issue of religious freedom is currently under review. In May 2018, an expert panel set up by the Australian Government to conduct a Religious Freedom Review presented its report. In response, the Government drafted a package of proposed legislation and initiated a public consultation process. Be aware that there may be changes to the law at the conclusion of the consultation period.

Each case is distinguished on its particular facts and the school will need to get advice before making a decision in any particular case.

The school can be held responsible for an act of discrimination by any of its staff or its volunteers. It is unlawful to victimise someone because they have made a complaint of discrimination.

Direct and indirect discrimination

Direct discrimination means treating someone less favourably than you would treat someone who does not have their attribute. For example, schools used to directly discriminate by allowing only boys to do trade subjects.

Direct discrimination also includes treating someone unfavourably because of a stereotyped notion about people with that attribute. For example, the statement, 'Boys lack the sensitivity to learn peer mediation skills' is based on stereotypes about males.

Table 3.1 Protected attributes under state and territory legislation

State	ACT	NSW	NT	QLD	SA	TAS	VIC	WA
Religious or political beliefs/activity or industrial activity	✓		✓	✓	✓	✓	✓	✓
Race	✓	✓	✓	✓	✓	✓	✓	✓
Transgender or gender identity or gender history	✓	✓	✓	✓	✓	✓	✓	✓
Marital or domestic status	✓	✓	✓	✓	✓	✓	✓	✓
Pregnancy			✓	✓	✓	✓	✓	✓
Breastfeeding or associations with a child	✓	✓	✓	✓		✓	✓	✓
Disability or physical impairment	✓	✓	✓	✓	✓	✓	✓	✓
Physical features							✓	
Age	✓	✓	✓	✓	✓	✓	✓	✓
Sex	✓	✓	✓	✓	✓	✓	✓	✓
Sexuality/sexual orientation/ homosexuality	✓	✓	✓	✓	✓	✓	✓	✓

Discrimination

State	ACT	NSW	NT	QLD	SA	TAS	VIC	WA
Lawful sexual activity			✓	✓		✓	✓	
HIV/AIDS	✓	✓						
Spent or irrelevant criminal convictions	✓		✓			✓		✓
Irrelevant medical record				✓		✓		
Family or carer responsibilities	✓	✓		✓	✓	✓	✓	✓
Association with a person having one of the attributes	✓		✓	✓			✓	✓

Indirect discrimination occurs where an unreasonable requirement is made that it is more difficult for people with a particular attribute to comply with. Examples include unreasonably specifying a minimum height for an activity (this might exclude girls and people of some ethnic backgrounds). A less obvious form of indirect discrimination would be providing extracurricular activities, sport or excursions only at times when it is difficult for students from particular cultural or religious groups to attend.

In a recent case, a school was found to have indirectly discriminated against a deaf student when the school failed to provide adequate Auslan interpretation. The school had not refused to enrol the student, but had wanted the student to pursue an educational program that was not based on Auslan interpretation.[1]

Coeducational schools might discriminate unlawfully if they have different standards of dress, appearance, or behaviour for boys and girls. In Victoria, schools may set reasonable standards of dress, appearance and behaviour, such as standards that take into account the views of the school community.

Disability standards for education

In August 2005, detailed Disability Standards for Education were introduced by the Federal Government to make more explicit for schools their obligations under disability discrimination laws. The standards set out the sorts of reasonable steps schools are expected to take to ensure that students with disabilities are provided with opportunities to realise their potential. Reasonable adjustments may need to be made to classrooms, curriculum and assessment so that the disabled student can participate in courses and programs. Special support services may need to be provided. In 2010, a Perth private school issued an apology in the Federal Magistrates Court as part of final settlement to a dispute brought by the parents of a student with autism spectrum disorder, who had been denied an aide. In the apology, the school admitted it had breached Western Australia's *Disability Discrimination Act 1992* and the Disability Standards for Education by failing to provide a trained educational assistant for the student.[2]

With the roll-out of the National Disability Insurance Scheme (NDIS), students who qualify for NDIS support may get access to assistive technology and therapy specific to their disability, but the school remains responsible for the adjustments needed to meet the requirements of the Disability Standards for Education, including modifications to buildings, teaching, learning assistance and transport between school activities. Schools can avoid complying with the standards where it would cause unjustifiable hardship. The fact that a school has to spend extra money to accommodate the needs of the disabled student/s would not necessarily be seen as an unjustifiable hardship by the courts.[3]

In assessing whether a school would be facing unjustifiable hardship, the court would take into account a range of factors, which balance the interests of all parties affected.

In *Walker v. State of Victoria*[4], the Federal Court discussed the standards required of a school and what is reasonable.

In some circumstances it may be reasonable for an educational institution to discriminate against a student with a disability to protect the health, safety or welfare of others. Students with autism spectrum disorder (ASD), attention deficit hyperactivity disorder (ADHD) and oppositional defiant disorder (ODD) can present schools with challenges and accusations of discrimination when a student is suspended, restrained or excluded from class. In a recent case[5], the Federal Court found that the Queensland Department of Education and Training had not discriminated against a student who had been diagnosed with ASD, ODD and ADHD on the occasions when the school suspended him, forcibly restrained him and withdrew him from the classroom to a withdrawal room. Having listened to the evidence, Justice Rangiah concluded that the student had not been treated less favourably than a student without his disability. The decisions to suspend him and withdraw him from class were the result of his behaviour, not his disability. Justice Rangiah also found that the physical restraint was proportional and reasonable, stating that if a student without disabilities 'had engaged in behaviour which similarly harmed or placed at risk of harm the student, other students or staff, then that student would also have been restrained'.

In deciding whether or not a school has unlawfully discriminated against a disabled student the court will look at the facts of each case. In the case discussed above, the Queensland Department of Education and Training was able to mount a successful defence largely because the school and the teachers had kept good records. It is essential that decisions are recorded (including the reasons for making decisions), that good minutes are kept at meetings and that teachers make contemporaneous notes. It is essential that schools become familiar with the Disability

Standards for Education. The standards and guidance notes can be found on the federal Department of Education website (see 'Directory', p. 158).

Harassment of students with disabilities

No defence of unjustifiable hardship can be used where a claim against the school involves harassment or victimisation of a student.

- The Disability Standards define 'harassment' as acts in relation to a student's disability that are reasonably likely to humiliate, offend, intimidate or distress the student or their helper.
- Victimisation occurs when someone has been treated unfairly for complaining or helping others to complain about an incident of discrimination or harassment.

Schools are required to develop programs in relation to harassment and victimisation of students with disabilities that will:

- inform staff and students of their obligation not to harass those students, or their helpers
- prevent such harassment and victimisation
- provide a mechanism for dealing with harassment or victimisation complaints.

Learning disabilities

A student who presents as a 'slow learner' may have a specific learning disability and should be assessed by an educational psychologist. If you become aware that a student has a learning disability, it could be indirect discrimination if you do not modify your teaching practice to take account of it. If a teacher's aide is needed for the student to learn effectively, you should bring the matter to the attention of the school administration (see 'Professional negligence', p. 109).

Discrimination and sport

Sex discrimination

Children under 12 may participate in all sports regardless of sex. If, however, an all-girls team were organised in a primary school to encourage more girls to play, this would not be discriminatory unless a boy wished to join and was not allowed to.

Once they reach age 12, students may be excluded on the basis of sex where the strength, stamina or physique of competitors is relevant.[6] This age is not an automatic cut-off point for girls, and the issue of strength, stamina and physique will vary from sport to sport. In a Victorian case, a judge determined that the differences between girls' and boys' strength, stamina and physique are not significant in the playing of Australian rules (AFL) football until girls reach 14.[7] Post-puberty girls can sensibly participate in contact sports with other girls. The number of girls and women playing AFL and soccer has risen significantly in recent years and there is now an AFL Women's competition. The Football Federation of Australia released census data in 2019, which showed that female players accounted for 22% of the soccer participants. However, where a girl wants to play on a boys' sports team, duty of care requires that she should only be permitted to do so if she has the size, strength and skill to match that of the boys she is playing with and against.

Impairment

In competitive sports, selection to participate may be based on skill or ability to do the sport. Accordingly, there will be some sports from which students with particular disabilities can be excluded. However, those students should still be given the opportunity to compete in other sports (see 'Disability Standards for Education', p. 88).

Age

Age-based sporting competitions are permissible.

Compulsory sport, physical education and outdoor education requiring students to participate in activities that are contrary to their religious beliefs may be indirect discrimination.

A school might also indirectly discriminate by requiring a student to participate in physical education or outdoor activities where that student does not want to because of a disability that makes the activity difficult. This includes a student with a subtle impairment, for example, requiring a student with a phobia about heights to go abseiling. This could also amount to a breach of the duty of care. This underlines the importance of physical education and outdoor education teachers having full medical histories of their students (see 'Duty of care', p. 5).

Sexual harassment

This should be read in conjunction with 'Physical contact and sexual assault' (p. 65).

It is unlawful for staff to sexually harass students or other staff at school (or at another educational institution with which the staff member is connected). Sexual harassment is broadly defined to include unwelcome sexual advances or conduct in which a reasonable person would anticipate that the other person would be offended, humiliated or intimidated. The sort of behaviour that can amount to unwelcome sexual conduct includes:

- unwelcome touching or kissing
- suggestive comments or jokes (oral, written, email, social networking) or inappropriate questions of a sexual nature
- displaying pictures of a sexual nature
- making sexual gestures.

Such a broad definition covers not only behaviour in private, but also the behaviour of teachers in the classroom.

The test of whether harassment has occurred is objective. This means that even if teachers do not believe they are harassing someone, it could still amount to harassment. Accordingly, when the curriculum requires matters of a sexual nature to be dealt with, teachers should exercise sensitivity when monitoring students' responses.

It is unlawful for students who have attained the age of 16 to harass staff or other students at school or at another educational institution to which the student is connected. (In the Australian Capital Territory, Queensland, Tasmania and Victoria, the age limit does not apply.)

Harassment policies

Schools should develop a harassment policy for staff and students, and ensure that everyone in the school is aware of its content. As well as sexual harassment, the policy should cover harassment because of disability (see 'Harassment of students with disabilities', p. 90), race, ethnicity, gender identity or any other of the attributes included in federal or state legislation.

Schools and principals can be liable for sexual harassment carried out by a staff member, including non-teaching staff, and by volunteers. However, a defence can be that reasonable precautions were taken to prevent the harassment, for example, having a well-publicised and effective harassment policy.

If you feel that the school is not attempting to protect you from sexual harassment by students, you should contact your union, a solicitor, a state or territory anti-discrimination agency or the Human Rights Commission.

CHECKLIST

- ☑ Schools should be familiar with the grounds of unlawful discrimination and have an anti-discrimination policy and an anti-harassment policy.
- ☑ You should be familiar with the unlawful grounds of discrimination.
- ☑ Discrimination based on stereotyped ideas is unlawful.
- ☑ Impairment discrimination is permissible in limited circumstances—check the Disability Standards for Education and the exemptions.
- ☑ Keep thorough records. When making a decision that may affect a student adversely, record the decision and the reasons why you came to that decision.
- ☑ Keep detailed minutes of any meetings with students, parents and staff.
- ☑ Religious schools may sometimes discriminate where it is necessary to avoid offending their religious beliefs.
- ☑ Particular sorts of discrimination in sport are permissible.
- ☑ Ignoring students' learning difficulties can amount to discrimination.
- ☑ You should be familiar with the definition of sexual harassment.

CONFIDENTIALITY, PRIVACY AND FREEDOM OF INFORMATION

Confidential information from students

Teachers are often told things by their students or colleagues in confidence. The general rule is that you should not disclose confidential information to others except in the following situations:
- Where a student may be at risk of sexual or physical abuse. Where a student is in danger of physical or sexual abuse, the law relating to mandatory reporting of child abuse will apply (see 'Reporting child abuse', p. 126).
- Where the student's physical or emotional health or safety is in danger. A confidential conversation with a student might reveal that the student is in a distressed state, has a medical or psychiatric condition, has a problem with substance abuse, or is in some other danger. If the student or their parents are not taking adequate steps to deal with the problem, you might have to take action that breaches the confidence (see 'Duty of care', p. 5).
- Where the student's condition creates a danger to others. Discuss the matter with the principal or student welfare staff member to devise a strategy, which may include notifying the police. In an emergency, contact the police immediately.

- When giving evidence in court. Teachers are required to answer questions truthfully and cannot refuse to answer because the information was received in confidence (see 'Appearing in court', p. 144).

When these difficult situations arise, you should act quickly and discuss the matter with the staff member responsible for student welfare, or the principal.

Privacy

Government schools

Government schools are not covered by the federal *Privacy Act 1988* but are subject to any state or territory privacy legislation or scheme covering the public sector. The strength of privacy protection varies from state to state. In Victoria, for example, government schools are required to protect personal information in accordance with the *Privacy and Data Protection Act 2014* (Vic) and the *Health Records Act 2001*. Similarly, in New South Wales, the *Privacy and Personal Information Protection Act 1998* and *Health Records and Information Privacy Act 2002* protect personal information collected by government schools. Queensland enacted the *Information Privacy Act* in 2009. Tasmania's privacy principles are set out in Schedule 1 of the *Personal Information Protection Act 2004* and South Australia has established Information Privacy Principles with complaints handled by a Privacy Committee. In Western Australia there is no legislative protection for privacy other than that provided by the state's *Freedom of Information Act 1992*. The Office of the Information Commissioner in the Northern Territory is responsible for overseeing the *Information Act 2002*, which contains some privacy protection and freedom of information. With respect to the collection, use and disclosure of personal information, the ACT Education Directorate is bound by the *Information Privacy Act 2014*.

In general, privacy laws provide that, where personal information about a student is received, it should only be disclosed for the purpose for which it was received, or with the student's or provider's consent, or where there is a threat to health or safety. For example, parents provide information about their child's health on the understanding that it will only be given to those who need to know it. Accordingly, the information could go to teachers who will be supervising the student on a camp or excursion, or to the classroom teacher where it is relevant to classroom behaviour or academic performance. In the case of a student at risk of anaphylaxis, the school should have a communication plan in place (see 'Anaphylaxis' p. 40). Sensitive personal information (e.g. about sexual preference, beliefs or health) should not be collected without the individual's consent.

Non-government schools

A non-government school's release of confidential information is likely to be a breach of contract (see 'Students as consumers', p. 110).

Prior to 12 March 2014, non-government schools were bound by the federal National Privacy Principles (NPP) set out in the *Privacy Act 1988*. The NPP has now been replaced by the Australian Privacy Principles (APPs) found in the federal *Privacy Amendment (Enhancing Privacy Protection) Act 2012* (Cth), and the *Privacy Amendment (Notifiable Data Breaches) Act 2017* (Cth), which commenced in February 2018. The *Privacy Amendment (Notifiable Data Breaches) Act 2017* (Cth) contains a section on how to respond to data breaches under the notifiable data breaches scheme. It is essential for schools to be aware that there are substantial penalties for serious or repeated interferences with privacy and the Office of the Australian Information Commissioner (OAIC) has the power to seek enforceable undertakings. A guide to the APPs can be found at the OAIC.[1] For those working in independent or Catholic schools, a privacy manual updated in November 2019 covering the legislation can be found online.[2]

The legislation requires schools to be open and transparent in their management of personal information and it is important that schools have an up-to-date privacy policy. The Act enhances the powers of the Privacy Commissioner and there is a greater emphasis on ensuring compliance. The Privacy Commissioner now has power to conduct assessments of privacy performance. In the case of serious or repeated breaches the OAIC may ask the court to impose a civil pecuniary penalty of up to $2.1 million per breach. Schools need to review their privacy policies, practices and procedures to ensure compliance with the APPs. Staff need to be informed and trained to implement the amended Act.

Under the APPs, the overriding principle is the open and transparent management of personal information. There are 13 APPs, which cover the same territory as the 10 NPPs, with some significant additions.

A non-government school must:
- only collect personal information that is necessary for its functions and activities. The person providing the information must be informed of the purpose of the collection, to whom the information will be disclosed, that they have a right to access their information collected by the school, how access will be provided and details of the complaints procedures including the right to complain to the Privacy Commissioner if the complaints procedure fails
- put in place procedures to handle unsolicited information (this is a new requirement)
- take special care when collecting sensitive information as detailed in the APPs. Sensitive information includes medical information and schools must take

extra care to obtain consent from the individual concerned and ensure protection of that information
- take care to ensure the personal information is of a high quality, accurate and up to date
- take reasonable steps to keep the information secure and destroy information that is no longer needed
- ensure that there is a system in place to collect, retain or destroy, store, manage and disclose information, and that the system is compliant with the Act as amended
- take extra care when using the cloud to store data to protect personal and sensitive information. Schools may be liable if there is leakage from an outsourced storage facility
- provide a clear, compliant privacy policy document that is open to the public
- provide a person with access to the information the school holds about them and take reasonable steps to correct inaccuracy (the Act as amended provides a limited range of circumstances under which access could be denied)
- ensure that an identifier of an individual issued by an Australian government agency is not used by the school as its own identifier of the individual, or disclosed
- where practicable, provide the individual with the option of remaining anonymous
- only allow overseas transfers of information under conditions set down by the APPs (the new legislation introduces new accountabilities to cross-border disclosure of information)
- provide a complaints procedure that is open and transparent
- appoint a Privacy Officer who has oversight of the system.

Schools and teachers are bound by strict privacy obligations and must take care to see that non-teaching staff and volunteers also understand these obligations.

Photographs

Photographs of students should only be used if consent has been obtained (general or specific).

General consent may be obtained by asking the parent to sign a standard collection notice giving consent to the use of their child's photograph by the school. The school should list the media where the photograph might appear and get the parent to tick each box. For example, a parent may consent to their child's photograph appearing in a school magazine or intranet but not on social media.

Specific consent is needed if the school wishes to use a photograph of a child in a situation not covered by the standard collection notice. A separate consent form, which covers the specific situation, needs to be signed by the parent.

If the student is over 15, they also need to sign the consent forms.

The student's right to make a decision on their own behalf

As a general principle, a young person is able to give consent when they are sufficiently mature and intelligent to understand what is being proposed. The guidelines on privacy in the public health sector stress that where a young person is capable of making their own decision with respect to personal information, they should be allowed to do so. Similar guidelines also give students the right to request information be withheld from their parents. Non-government schools can make the provision of reports, for example, a condition of their contract with parents, however this can become a grey area, particularly if a student over the age of 16 wishes to withhold information from their parents.

The *Privacy Act* sets no minimum age at which individuals can make a decision regarding their own personal information. The guidelines to the APPs suggest consideration on a case-by-case basis.

Freedom of information

The *Freedom of Information Act 1982* (FOI Act) provides a right of access to a range of federal government documents held by federal ministries and agencies. Each state and territory now has legislation equivalent to the FOI Act, thus extending access to information to state government institutions.

Freedom of information (FOI) laws aim to make government more accountable. Anyone, including a student, teacher, journalist, parent, lawyer or union, can make an FOI request from a government department, school or TAFE college. (The laws do not apply to information kept at non-government schools, but will apply to information, such as internally assessed grades, submitted by those schools to a government agency.) The department or school would then have to provide all documents in its possession on that topic (although some documents can be exempted). The term 'documents' includes formal reports, written notes, telephone messages, diary entries, minutes of meetings, tapes, photographs, drawings, film and digitally stored information. Whenever you write a report about a student or another teacher, care should be taken to ensure that the contents are accurate, as the report might be released later in response to an FOI request. Documents that are the subject of an FOI request may not be destroyed. You should avoid making or keeping unnecessary records relating to your students.

The education department, not the school, coordinates FOI requests. FOI law is very complex. If you are worried about the release of a document you have written, it might be possible to have it exempted. Seek the support of your school and education department, or obtain independent advice from your union or a lawyer.

If you want to make an FOI request for documents, contact the FOI officer in your education department.

CHECKLIST

- ☑ In general, information provided in confidence should not be disclosed to others without the consent of the person giving the information.
- ☑ Confidential information should be revealed where it concerns sexual or physical abuse, or where your duty of care requires it.
- ☑ Documents created in government schools may be subject to FOI requests.
- ☑ Government schools are required to apply the privacy legislation enacted in their state or territory.
- ☑ Non-government schools must apply the Australian Privacy Principles.
- ☑ Non-government schools should review their privacy policies to ensure that they are compliant with the Commonwealth *Privacy Amendment (Enhancing Privacy Protection) Act 2012* (Cth) and the *Privacy Amendment (Notifiable Data Breaches) Act 2017* (Cth).

DEFAMATION

Uniform defamation laws have applied throughout Australia since 2006.

What is defamation?
Defamation is saying or publishing something that damages a person's reputation. The publication can be in any format—letters, emails, internet sites, social media, film, cartoons, newspapers, radio, television and theatrical performances. It is not just words that can defame, but also the way people are depicted in photographs, films, theatrical or other performances.

Damage to reputation
To be defamatory, a statement must do more than just embarrass someone or hurt their feelings. It must damage their reputation in the eyes of 'reasonable' people. So if one of the school's teachers is depicted as an alcoholic in a school revue, this could be defamatory, as reasonable people would question the professional competence of a teacher with a drinking problem.

Innuendo, imputation and 'reading between the lines'
Sometimes a statement or picture that might appear on the surface to be harmless can still be defamatory, if it is intended to imply something damaging to a reputation. The maker of the statement might be leaving it to the reader to 'draw the obvious conclusion' or to 'read between the lines'. For example, a teacher intending to

criticise another teacher's work might say sarcastically that 'Mr Jones was managing his class with his usual standard of competence'.

To determine whether there is some intended defamatory innuendo in the statement, the courts will look at how an ordinary or reasonable recipient of the statement would read it. It is uncommon for teachers to be sued for defamation.

However, threats of defamation actions are sometimes made, and teachers themselves can sometimes be defamed by, and also themselves make defamatory statements about, students, parents, colleagues or school administrators.

Defences to defamation

Where you make a statement that damages someone's reputation, you will not be liable for defamation if one of the available defences applies. Consequently, what you say or publish will not lead to liability in the following circumstances.

Truth

No finding of defamation can be made if the statement is true or substantially true.

Contextual truth

There will be no liability if untrue defamatory material does no further harm to the victim when contained in a publication that contains other communications that are substantially true and that damage the victim's reputation.

Qualified privilege

The defence of qualified privilege will protect the statement if it is made:
- without malice (i.e. honestly)
- to someone who should be given that information because it is relevant to their particular job, or

position or responsibilities they have (i.e. they have a legitimate interest in receiving that information)
- it is reasonable to make the statement.

An example would be that a teacher reports to the principal that they believe a student has cheated in a test, or that a colleague has behaved improperly. If their statement is subsequently found to be untrue, the maker of the statement will not be liable if they acted honestly and it was reasonable to make the statement (i.e. the defence of qualified privilege will apply).

Similarly, the defence will apply where a teacher has been asked to write a reference, or to appraise someone's work, and their comments include critical statements. Provided they are reasonable and not made for malicious purposes, and the person to whom they are published has an interest in receiving them, then liability for defamation will not be incurred.

The defence also applies to defamatory statements in student reports, provided the statements are made reasonably and without malice (i.e. honestly).

Sometimes a teacher will discuss a student's parents with a colleague, to help understand the student's behaviour. Criticism of the parents in this context is not defamatory if it is made honestly. The teacher's colleague will have a legitimate interest in receiving that information as it will assist them in teaching or managing that student.

On the other hand, passing on gossip about a colleague, parent or student to someone who does not need to have that information to assist them to carry out their responsibilities or to do their job could lose the protection of qualified privilege. Hence if the statement proves to be untrue, it could lead to liability for defamation.

One factor that can be taken into account when determining whether it is reasonable to pass on the information is the extent to which steps were taken to verify the information. If wild accusations are passed on without attempting to check their accuracy, the protection of qualified privilege could be lost.

Fair comment
If the statement is fair comment, there can be no liability for defamation. This means that it is an honestly held opinion on a matter of public interest. This is the defence that protects newspaper reviews of public events or of artistic works, such as films and plays. The defence fails if the opinion is not honest, or if it is based on facts that are not substantially true.

Not publicising a comment
If you criticise someone to their face, or in a private and confidential document sent to them, and you do not repeat or allow someone else to see the statement, it will not amount to defamation. Defamation law aims to protect reputation, and reputation will only be damaged where you communicate the information to a third person.

School plays, publications, films and the internet
School publications, productions and internet sites provide potential ways for students (and staff) to disseminate defamatory statements. Accordingly, a close eye should be kept on them. Anyone involved in the dissemination of such statements could be liable, including the writer, editors, teachers assisting the production and the school.

However, if a comment, such as a review of a play or film, is an honest expression of opinion on a matter of public interest and the opinion is based on facts, the comment will not be defamatory, as the defence of fair comment (mentioned above) will apply.

As mentioned earlier, someone can be defamed through innuendo, and not just through a direct statement.

Accordingly, if someone is not named, for example, in an article, a play, or a film, it could still be defamatory if they can be identified by the circumstances or context. To be defamatory, a statement must do more than just embarrass someone or hurt their feelings. It must damage their reputation in the eyes of 'reasonable' people (see 'Damage to reputation', p. 103).

Defamation insurance

If the school or student publications do include controversial articles, the school's insurance cover should be investigated to see if it covers monetary loss from defamation actions.

Finally, legal proceedings are very expensive, so you need to carefully consider advice from your union or lawyer before you become involved in defamation proceedings.

Social media

The increasing popularity of social media sites has provided a medium for defamatory comments on teachers and school principals by students and parents. Despite the costs, teachers who believe their reputations have been destroyed by social media have taken court action as a last resort. In 2012, a former school principal was awarded $40 000 by an Adelaide Magistrates Court over a defamatory Facebook page created by parents of her students.[1] In one of the first judgments involving defamation via Twitter, a former student who posted defamatory statements against his music teacher was ordered to pay $105 000 in damages, plus costs in the New South Wales District Court.[2] In 2020, Southport District Court in Queensland found that the principal of Tamborine Mountain High School had been defamed by parent comments on Facebook and awarded her $6000 in damages.[3]

CHECKLIST

- ☑ Ensure that comments in a report or reference are true.
- ☑ Carefully examine your motives when making a negative report or evaluation about someone.
- ☑ If you are making a statement that will damage someone's reputation, question whether you are under a duty to make the statement, and whether the person to whom you are making the statement has a legitimate interest in receiving it.
- ☑ Check that material in a school play, revue, magazine or newspaper is not defamatory.
- ☑ If students are using email in your class, ensure that they are using their school email account and they are aware that you can monitor what they are writing through the school system administrators.

PROFESSIONAL NEGLIGENCE

Schools are not about to be inundated with claims for professional negligence, despite some teachers' fears. In the United States the courts have refused to consider such claims, and in Australia the small number of claims are usually settled out of court.

The law in this area is still unclear, as the courts have not yet had to decide major cases setting out the scope of school and teacher liability. However, on the basis of Australian consumer protection laws, and cases from here and the United Kingdom, it seems that liability for professional negligence could arise where:
- a teacher carelessly gives advice or makes statements
- a teacher carelessly carries out specific duties
- a school is careless in identifying learning difficulties
- a school that accepts fees fails to provide the level or quality of service promised or expected under the contract, or required by consumer protection laws.

For a negligence action to succeed, however, the student has to have suffered some actual or potential financial loss, and this could be difficult to prove. Sensible, careful teaching will ensure that you avoid trouble.

Careless advice and statements

Any teacher who makes a statement or gives advice to someone on a serious matter is required to take care when making it, where they know that the person will rely on and act on that statement. If a statement or advice proves to be incorrect, but you made appropriate investigations and thought carefully before making it, then you will not have committed professional negligence.

Making factual statements and giving advice are central to teaching. You should take care that what you are teaching is correct. For example, it could be professional negligence if the wrong books were taught for an English examination, or a component from an out-of-date Year 12 study design was taught.

Similarly, care should be taken when advising students on subject choice and careers. Tell the student to check with the appropriate university handbook or tertiary admissions handbook, or the careers teacher, with regard to prerequisite subjects and admissions procedures.

You should limit advice to your areas of professional competence, and areas for which you are responsible.

Careless performance of tasks

While there are no court decisions in this area, you are probably under a duty of care when carrying out particular tasks such as the internal assessment of Year 12 students' work and submission of marks to the government assessment authority (see 'Duty of care', p. 5).

Identifying learning difficulties

Court cases in the United Kingdom have decided that teachers are under a duty to act carefully when identifying and dealing with students' learning difficulties. This does not mean that all teachers have to become educational psychologists. However, you should observe your students' progress sufficiently carefully to identify anyone experiencing difficulties, and report problems to the person responsible for special education or to the principal.

Students as consumers

When schools accept a fee for their services, a legally enforceable contract is created between the school and the person who paid the fee (usually a parent or guardian). Enrolment in a non-government school creates a contract, as does enrolment of a fee-paying overseas student in a government school. Charging parents of government school students a fee for additional courses, such as software courses or swimming lessons, or for a camp or excursion, creates a contract in relation to that particular activity. Where a school fails to carry out a specific contractual promise that it made to the parents or students, it might be in breach of its contract and liable for any financial loss the parent has suffered. Examples of this could be where a non-government school fails to provide the remedial education it promised for students encountering literacy difficulties, or where a government school fails to provide the activities promised, and paid for by a parent, on a camp or excursion.

Liability under contract and consumer protection laws is incurred by the school, not by individual teachers. However, where a teacher's carelessness is responsible for the school not fulfilling its contractual obligation, the teacher might have failed in their obligations as an employee, and be in danger of dismissal.

CHECKLIST

- ☑ Keep up with changes to compulsory curriculum.
- ☑ Ensure that factual material being taught is correct.
- ☑ Take care when assessing work and reporting results.
- ☑ Take care when advising students.
- ☑ Schools should ensure that a prospectus or contractual document does not promise anything the school cannot deliver.
- ☑ If you are asked to teach in an area outside of your professional expertise, you should insist on training to increase your knowledge and skills.
- ☑ Report any suspected student learning difficulties to the responsible teacher or the principal.

COPYRIGHT

Copyright is the legal protection given to a 'work' that someone has created. This could be an article, book or manual, musical piece, artistic work, sculpture, film, video, television or radio broadcast, computer program or work published on the internet. The work does not have to be marked with the traditional © symbol—the act of creating the work gives rise to copyright in Australia. Copyright protects the author's entitlement to profits from their labour and the publisher's entitlement to a return for the expense of publication. Two excellent starting points for information about copyright are:
- the National Copyright Guidelines, which have been produced through a joint activity, *Smartcopying*, undertaken by the state and territory education departments and non-government school authorities (see 'Directory', p. 160)
- the Australian Copyright Council (see 'Directory', p. 157).

Who owns copyright?

Generally, the person who creates the work owns the copyright and is entitled to prevent anyone else reproducing or communicating the work without their permission. The author or creator can sell copyright to someone else. For example, authors of books and songwriters may sell or licence the copyright to the publisher, and receive royalties in exchange. The copyright in written materials produced as part of your teaching duties (e.g. curriculum design and support material) belongs to your employer. However, copyright in a book written largely in your spare time would not normally belong to your employer.

Expiry of copyright

Copyright used to exist for 50 years after the death of the creator. Since January 2005, copyright exists for 70 years after the death of the creator unless it had already expired by January 2005. From 1 January 2019, unpublished works are subject to the same expiry rules as published works. For government publications, copyright still lasts for 50 years after publication.

Where the works of, say, Mozart or Shakespeare have been published, the publisher still owns copyright in that particular published edition of the work, with its particular typographical arrangement, for 25 years from publication. The publisher does not own copyright in the content of the edition, but has rights regarding reproducing that particular edition (by photocopying, making an electronic copy, etc.).

Creating a website

If you are creating a website and placing on it works created by other people, permission should be obtained from the copyright holders.

Permissible copying for educational purposes

Several licensing schemes operate to allow schools to make and use copies of works for educational purposes (but not for profit). All government and Catholic schools and most independent schools are permitted a certain amount of photocopying or electronic copying of written material and music, electronic text and graphics (including notated music) and the taping of television and radio broadcasts, for use in the classroom. A licence fee is paid to the Copyright Agency Limited (CAL) and to Screenrights (see 'Directory', p. 158 and 160), which pay remuneration to copyright owners. A copy made under the Screenrights licence must include a statement that the material has been copied and communicated pursuant to the statutory licence in section 113P of the *Copyright Act*.

For full details on permissible copying by schools or if your school is not licensed under these schemes, contact the Australian Copyright Council (see 'Directory', p. 157).

Copying printed and electronic form material

The entire work may be copied in electronic or hard form if:
- you have the copyright owner's permission
- it is an article in a periodical
- it is fewer than 15 pages published in an anthology
- it is not separately published
- the work is not currently available at an ordinary commercial price.

Otherwise, 10 per cent of the words (or bars of music) may be copied, or one chapter if the work is divided into chapters. If the work is in electronic form only, a reasonable portion is 10% of the total number of words. Copied material may be communicated to students or staff electronically (e.g. via email or online) for educational purposes.

The 'moral rights' obligation (see p. 116) to the creator requires that the name of the creator of a work appears on the copied material.

Material reproduced in electronic form must contain a particularly worded statement advising that any further copying might infringe copyright.

Artistic works within other works

All artistic works within an article or other work (i.e. still images, such as illustrations in a book or PDF, but not animated images) may be copied wherever it is permitted to copy the containing work.

Copying music

The Australasian Mechanical Copyright Owners Society (AMCOS) issues the licences that permit schools to photocopy sheet music for educational purposes. Education department licences cover government schools, while non-government schools need to opt in through their governing organisations. You can contact AMCOS for their free booklet and details of what is permitted (see 'Directory', p. 158).

AMCOS and the Australian Recording Industry Association (ARIA) can also jointly license the reproduction of certain video and audio recordings of music (see 'Directory', p. 158).

Performing rights

A literary, dramatic or musical work can be performed in the classroom as part of educational instruction. Otherwise, permission to perform a play should be obtained from the play's publisher and/or a fee paid, unless copyright has expired. Public performance of music is permissible if it is under a licence from the Australasian Performing Rights Association (APRA) (see 'Directory', p. 158). Parents and schools may record the performance provided the APRA licence permits it. Copies of the recording of a performance may be provided to students and parents of the school and the school may recover the costs involved but must not make a profit.

Before filming a performance, the school should make sure that permissions have been obtained from all those who will be photographed (to adhere with privacy guidelines) and from the performers who need to consent to the filming of their performance (to comply with performers' rights). Note that since July 2007 performers also have moral right to their work under amendments to the *Copyright Act 1968*. The rules regarding making sound recordings of performances are more complicated, and AMCOS should be contacted about this.

APRA licences do not cover performance of musicals or operas. In those cases the school should contact the music publisher or their agent. The Australian Copyright Council has details of the main agents (see 'Directory', p. 157).

Moral rights

The creator has certain moral rights associated with their work, which include:
- having the integrity of the work respected and not having it subjected to derogatory treatment
- being attributed for the work.

Clear and reasonably prominent attribution must be given to the creator of any work that is reproduced as part of the school's activities.

Recording television, cable and radio programs

Most schools come under the Statutory Broadcast Licence through which payments are made to Screenrights (see 'Directory', p. 160), for the use of radio and television broadcasts. The licence permits recording radio and television programs for educational purposes (but not for profit), as long as the copies are marked with particular information. Copies can be communicated to students for educational purposes via a website, ClickView or an email and must include a notice along the following lines:

> *This material has been copied [and communicated to you] in accordance with the statutory licence in section 113P of the Copyright Act. Any further reproduction or communication of this material by you may be the subject of copyright protection under the Act. Do not remove this notice.*

The licence covers all free-to-air broadcasts but does not cover streaming services such as Netflix. If you record material from a streaming service such as Netflix you may be covered by section 28 provided the use is solely educational, or under Section AB, which covers the flexible dealing exception. The *Copyright Amendment (Disability Access and Other Measures) Act 2017* provides some protection from legal liability provided you can show that you took reasonable steps to reduce copyright infringement.

Screening films

Films (including hired ones) may be shown in class unless the hire agreement prohibits screening outside the home. However, they cannot be streamed over the internet or copied, or an admission fee charged to view them. Pirated copies of films may not be shown.

Video hosting sites

The general rule is that you can stream from YouTube and other video hosting sites in class, but you are not allowed to download the work and make copies. If the video has an embed code, you can embed the video into your course materials. It is also safe to provide a link.

Members of TeacherTube are allowed to download videos for use in the classroom for educational use only, provided there is a link back to TeacherTube in any media in which the downloaded video is used. (Read the terms and conditions before downloading.)

Computer programs

You may not copy a computer program without the copyright owner's permission. You may make a backup copy for yourself, unless the copyright owner has expressly forbidden this. Some software is purchased with a licence permitting its installation on a school network.

Copying from USBs or other storage devices
The content licence will indicate the legal obligations attached to the licence, for example, whether it can be made available over a network.

Copying from the internet for educational purposes
Material on the internet is also protected by copyright. If it is pirated material you will infringe copyright if you copy it. However, you may copy:
- any material that the owner gives permission to copy
- material mentioned on p. 114 under 'Copying printed and electronic form material'.

Schools are able to temporarily cache entire websites to enable students to access them more efficiently for educational purposes (proxy caching). This avoids any problem flowing from all students in a class simultaneously downloading from the same site.

AMCOS/ARIA licences do not permit reproductions of sound recordings downloaded from unauthorised internet sites (i.e. pirated material).

Format-shifting
Format-shifting involves copying content from one format to another, for example, making a DVD copy of a VHS tape of a film, converting a film to MP4 or converting audio files to a digital format such as MP3.

The general rule is that schools cannot copy films, sound recordings, games or software if making a copy involves circumventing an access control technology. The *Copyright Act* prohibits the circumvention of the technological protection measure (TPM). However, if the work falls short of being TPM protected (regional coding, for example, is not a TPM) the school may be able to copy it into another format if a case can be made under the 'flexible dealing' provisions under Section 200AB. Further copying exceptions were enacted in the 2017 amendments.[1] Under

these provisions, a school or TAFE college is allowed to format-shift copyright material if:
- the original copy is lawful (i.e. not pirated)
- the copy will only be used for educational instruction
- it is not possible to buy the work in the new format within a reasonable time
- the format-shifted copy will not be used in a way that would unreasonably prejudice the copyright owner (e.g. giving students access to an electronic copy that they could copy)
- making the format-shifted copy does not involve removing or disabling a TPM.

People with disabilities

Special provisions apply to the copying of material for people with print or intellectual disabilities. *The Copyright Amendment (Disability Access and Other Measures) Act 2017* extended the fair dealing exception for persons with disability, allowing the school or TAFE to make accessible copies of necessary educational materials in a format not otherwise available to the student. There is no restriction on the kind of format that can be created. The school is also allowed to circumvent the technological protection measure (TPM) if this is necessary to allow access for the student with a disability. Contact the Australian Copyright Council for details (see 'Directory', p. 157).

Copying by students

Students can copy material for research and study, provided the copying is 'fair'. Fairness includes all of an article, or 10 per cent or one chapter of a book, dramatic or musical work, or website.

Schools can be liable if staff instruct students to make copies that will infringe copyright. The *Copyright Act* as amended (Section 39A) provides that a school library will not be held to have authorised the making of an infringing copy by reason only that the copy was made on a machine belonging to the library, so long as copyright warning notices are installed. Warning notices must be placed in close proximity to the machines and clearly visible to the person using the machine and must be in accordance with the prescribed dimensions and form. For the format for the warning notices see Australian Copyright Council Information sheet 'Notices on photocopiers and other copying equipment'.[2]

The school will still be liable if the school is seen to have authorised the infringement and may be held vicariously liable for the actions of its staff.

Strictly educational use

Schools, teachers and students are allowed greater freedom to copy for educational purposes and have licences that allow them to do so. It is important that such copying that does take place is strictly limited to educational purposes and not open to the public. This means that course materials that contain copyright material will need to be password-protected. Similarly, films that are shown for educational purposes cannot be shown for recreational purposes.

Students may use copyright material in their school projects but will not be able to enter such projects into public competitions. If the school, teacher or student wishes to make their work more widely available there is an increasing amount of material being made available under open licence schemes.

Creative Commons

Open licences such as Creative Commons (CC) permit the reproduction and communication of works (text, music, film images, etc.) without having to ask the copyright owner for permission, provided you are using the work within the terms of the licence. CC provide six options within their standard licence. You may be allowed to adapt or modify the work; however, any creative changes that you have made may have to be made available to others under an open licence. Any material used under CC must attribute the creator of the work.[3]

Australian Copyright Council legal advice

The Australian Copyright Council provides a free online legal advice service to staff of educational institutions (except state schools in Queensland, who have been referred to in-house lawyers). The service is limited to questions that cannot be answered using the information sheets provided.

Impact of COVID-19

The spread of COVID-19 brought about the closure of most school classrooms in Australia with lessons being delivered online. While online learning is not new, the delivery of all lessons online highlighted copyright issues with respect to digital technology. For some time, the education sector has been pushing for changes to copyright law so as to allow educators greater flexibility in a digital economy. In 2013, the Australian Law Reform Commission recommended amendments to copyright legislation to give greater flexibility to the education sector. The *Copyright Amendment (Disability Access and Other Measures) Act 2017* provided increased access for students with disabilities and extended and simplified the licensing and exemptions under the legislation. In August 2020, the federal government announced that it will proceed with further copyright reform, which will provide greater flexibility to educational institutions.[4]

In response to the COVID-19 pandemic, the Copyright Agency produced guidelines for teachers and educational institutions, including special arrangements allowing teachers to read storybooks online. These special arrangements were for the duration of the COVID-19 emergency only.[5]

Even after the virus has been brought under control it is likely that online delivery will increasingly be utilised as an effective learning mechanism. It is likely that there will be further changes to copyright law to bring Australia in line with the USA and UK, In the meantime, teachers are advised to:
- provide links or embed content rather than copy
- use free resources (Creative Commons, licensed material and open-education resources)
- only make content available to the students who need it
- ensure that the material cannot be copied or downloaded
- remove access to the material after a reasonable period
- protect access to virtual classes with usernames and passwords.

CHECKLIST

- ☑ The person who creates a work generally owns the copyright in it, and generally that work cannot be copied without permission.
- ☑ Most schools have licences that permit them to copy certain amounts of material for educational purposes only.
- ☑ There are rules governing performance rights for plays and music.
- ☑ Place copyright warning notices close to photocopiers, scanners and computers.
- ☑ Ensure that a copyright statement accompanies all copies made under the Screenrights licence.
- ☑ Do not format-shift unless you can make a clear case under provision 200AB or other provisions provided under the amended legislation
- ☑ You are allowed to circumvent a TPM to allow access to a student with a disability under the provisions of *The Copyright Amendment (Disability Access and Other Measures) Act 2017.*
- ☑ Make sure that everything copied is for educational use only.
- ☑ Follow the information provided by the Australian Copyright Council.
- ☑ Watch out for further copyright legislative reform.

PART 4

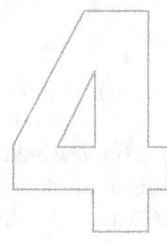

Welfare, family and crime

REPORTING CHILD ABUSE

In all Australian jurisdictions, teachers are mandated to make a report to the relevant authorities if they have formed a belief on reasonable grounds that a child has been, or is being, abused, or if the child is at risk of abuse. In New South Wales, the duty applies to children under 16 years of age, and in Victoria, the duty applies to children under 17 years of age. In the other states and territories, the duty applies to all children up to the age of 18. Sexual abuse can include penetrative and non-penetrative sexual activity and exposure to pornography.

Similarly, teachers in all jurisdictions (except Western Australia) are mandated to report physical abuse. As regards psychological or emotional abuse and child neglect, only teachers in New South Wales, South Australia, Tasmania and the Northern Territory are subject to a mandatory duty to report their reasonable suspicions. In New South Wales, suspected abuse is referred to as 'reportable conduct'.

In cases where a teacher is not mandated to report certain types of abuse but does so anyway, such a teacher has legal protection from a civil action where the report is made honestly and reasonably. In the Northern Territory and Tasmania, volunteers are also required to report. In Victoria, all adults have a legal duty to report child sexual abuse if they form a suspicion on reasonable grounds.

You do not have to provide proof of abuse—it is sufficient that you have reasonable grounds on which to base your belief. Failure to report could incur a fine.

In states where reporting a particular form of abuse is not mandatory or is limited, the school's and teacher's duty of care may still require staff to act where a student's behaviour suggests that the student might be experiencing abuse (see 'Duty of care', p. 5). Such suspected cases should be brought to the attention of, and followed up with, the principal or staff member responsible for student welfare.

Table 4.1 on p. 128 is provided as a guide only. You are advised to contact the relevant department or organisation to clarify the reporting requirements for your state or territory.

How to report

Where you suspect child abuse, it is not your role to investigate further. You should consult the designated teacher or counsellor at the school, the principal, or the state or territory community services or child welfare department (the name of the department varies from state to state; see 'Directory', p. 161).

If you have informed the designated person at the school about the suspected abuse and the matter has been reported to the relevant government department, then your responsibility is discharged. However, as it is your personal responsibility to report suspected child abuse, you should check that the report has been made.

If you are not satisfied that the school has acted on your reported suspicions, you should contact the community services or child welfare department directly. You do not need the school's permission to make a report and you should make a further report any time you have reasonable grounds for believing that further abuse has occurred.

Table 4.1 Mandatory reporting requirements for those working in Australian schools

Jurisdiction	Those mandated	State of mind	Abuse to be reported
ACT	• teacher at a school • nurse • counsellor at a school	• belief on reasonable grounds	• physical abuse • sexual abuse
NSW	• any manager, professional or other paid employee delivering services to children including education, health, welfare and residential services	• suspects on reasonable grounds that a child is at risk of significant harm	• physical abuse • sexual abuse • emotional/psychological abuse • neglect • exposure to domestic violence
NT	• any person	• belief on reasonable grounds	• physical abuse • sexual abuse • emotional/psychological abuse • neglect • exposure to domestic violence

QLD	• teachers	• becomes aware, or reasonably suspects	• sexual abuse • physical abuse
	• all school staff		• sexual abuse • (reporting of other abuse is not mandatory unless you are a teacher)
SA	• teachers in educational institutions • registered and enrolled nurses • psychologists	• suspects on reasonable grounds	• physical abuse • sexual abuse • emotional/psychological abuse • neglect
TAS	• principals and teachers in any educational institution • nurses • registered psychologists • anyone employed or volunteering in a government agency providing education, health or welfare services to children	• believes, or suspects, on reasonable grounds, or has knowledge that the child has been abused or neglected	• physical abuse • sexual abuse • emotional/psychological abuse • neglect • exposure to domestic violence

Continued …

Jurisdiction	Those mandated	State of mind	Abuse to be reported
VIC	• registered teachers and those with permission to teach • school principals • registered nurses	• belief on reasonable grounds	• physical abuse • sexual abuse
	• all adults	• belief on reasonable grounds	• sexual abuse • (reporting other abuse is not mandatory unless you are a teacher, school principal or nurse)
WA	• teachers • nurses	• belief on reasonable grounds	• sexual abuse

Reasonable grounds
Schools usually have guidelines for dealing with child abuse. You need to be familiar with these. The school may have a recording system for behaviour that seems abnormal to you and causes you concern.

There may be a number of indicators over a period of time, rather than a single indicator, which gives you reasonable grounds for believing that abuse has occurred. You should keep notes recording your observations, including indicators, dates and so on. These should not be kept as personal property, but should be made part of the official school records.

Consequences of reporting
Teachers cannot be liable in any legal proceedings for reporting suspected child abuse if the report was made in good faith, that is, it was made because they believed they had reasonable grounds for suspecting abuse.

If the community services or child welfare department believes there is risk of harm to the child, it might provide support and counselling for the family, or take action to remove the child from the family. The police may prosecute if a criminal offence is suspected, and they might interview teachers and the child.

Confidentiality
The fact that the notifier is a teacher will not be revealed unless you give consent. If court proceedings eventuate, your identity might be revealed, or you might be called to be a witness.

The Royal Commission into Institutional Responses to Child Sex Abuse
In December 2017, the Royal Commission into Institutional Responses to Child Sex Abuse presented its report after five years of inquiry, tabling 409 recommendations. Many of

these recommendations are directed to state and territory governments to introduce legislation to protect children in schools and in other government-run and non-government institutions. The Royal Commission urged the federal government to work with the states and territories to adopt uniform legislation in the areas of child protection and reporting. In response, the federal government established the National Office for Child Safety in July 2018, to develop a national strategy to prevent child sexual abuse and to report progress to the Prime Minister. There are now Child Safe Principles, which are recommended to be embedded into the culture of schools. These national principles are similar to the Child Safe Standards the Victorian government introduced into Victorian schools in 2016 that are now compulsory for all Victorian schools. Standard 5 covers procedures for responding to and reporting suspected child abuse.

In addition to the mandatory requirement for teachers to report child abuse, Victoria enacted a new criminal offence that could be applied to school principals or other members of staff in positions of authority. The offence, 'Failure by a person in authority to protect a child from a sexual offence' (*Crimes Act 1958* section 490) commenced on 1 July 2015.[1] This applies to the principal or any other person in authority, who has the power to protect a child from child abuse and fails to act. The offence carries a maximum penalty of five years in prison.

The Royal Commission also recommended that all jurisdictions introduce an offence of 'failure to protect'. In 2018, New South Wales strengthened its child protection legislation to include an offence of 'failure to protect', which would apply where a school employed a person who was clearly a risk to a child and the person in authority who had the power to remove the risk failed to do so. In 2019, the Queensland Department of Justice proposed amendments to their Criminal Code to include the offence of failing to protect a child from sexual abuse.

Although the states are moving towards uniform protection and reporting requirements, there are still substantial differences, as can be seen in the reporting requirements in Table 4.1.

CHECKLIST

- ☑ Keep a copy of the school's guidelines on responding to and reporting suspicions of child abuse.
- ☑ Become aware of the indicators of child abuse.
- ☑ Attend all training sessions.
- ☑ Keep up to date with the recommendations and resources at the National Office of Child Safety.
- ☑ If you have reported suspected child abuse, check that the school has passed your report on to the community services or child welfare department.
- ☑ If the school has not reported the suspected child abuse, you should report your suspicions to the appropriate department.
- ☑ Keep notes, making sure that you are recording facts and observations, not opinions.

FAMILY LAW PROBLEMS

Family law problems are difficult to deal with because they are highly emotive. The role of the school and the teacher is to act in accordance with the legal rights and obligations of the parents and children, not to make judgements on family law matters. However, the school and the teacher have a duty of care to the child and are responsible for the educational development of the child while enrolled at the school.

Who has legal control over a child?

Both parents of a child share equally the duties, responsibilities and authority with respect to rearing their child, regardless of whether the parents are married, living in a de facto relationship or separated. These parental rights can only be changed by a court order. While step-parents usually carry out a parenting role with a child, they do not automatically have legal parental rights; a court order is required to give them those rights.

When disputes arise

You may sometimes receive conflicting instructions from separated parents. You need to communicate equally with both parents and inform them when such difficulties arise.

You should take great care where a dispute has become particularly bitter, and avoid taking sides. All schools should have guidelines on family law disputes and you need to be familiar with these. You can also get advice from your union or the education department.

School reports, notices and excursions

Schools should send both separated parents copies of school reports and other school information, unless an order has been made restricting parental responsibility. Similarly, both parents should have access to teachers to discuss their children's progress unless a court orders otherwise.

Where parents cannot agree about a child attending an excursion, the school can comply with the wishes of the parent with whom the court has ordered the child should live (see 'Court orders', below).

Court orders

In most cases separated parents agree about living and contact arrangements for the child, with both parents retaining joint responsibility for the child. When the parties cannot agree, either the Family Court or the Federal Circuit Court can make an order specifying with whom the child is to live and what time the other parent may spend with the child. The parent with whom the child is to live can make day-to-day decisions about the child, while decisions on long-term issues (e.g. which school to attend) are usually up to both parents, unless the court orders otherwise.

The practice in many schools is for the principal to ask (in writing if necessary) to see a copy of the court order, which has the court's seal stamped on it, and then a copy of the order can be made for the school files. The school is then prepared should one parent arrive at the school unexpectedly, either to see the child or to try to take the child away unlawfully. The school can point out that it cannot assist a parent to breach a court order.

If the school has sighted a court order, it is also prepared should one parent maliciously allege that the school should not allow the other parent any access to the school. Court orders can be changed, so the principal needs to be sure that the school has the latest version. Where a court order has not been made the principal can ask the parents to confirm the arrangements for the children in writing.

School's duty of care

You should exercise care if a parent arrives at the school to see or take a child, and the child becomes distressed or states that they do not want to see the parent. You should take the matter to the principal, assistant principal or senior person responsible for student welfare. They may know about the existence of a court order or the background to the dispute, and will have access to legal advice should it be necessary. They can also telephone the parent with whom the school normally has contact, in order to find out if it is appropriate to release the child to the other parent.

If that parent cannot be contacted, the principal can ask to see a court order authorising the parent's contact with the child. If necessary, a call can be made to the Family Court or Federal Circuit Court to check on the order.

You should not give a student's home address to a separated parent and should advise the parent to see the principal. Schools can be in a difficult position because of the duty of care they owe to their students. They need to be sure that they are not releasing a child into a dangerous situation. On the other hand, they cannot interfere with a parent who is exercising legitimate rights. If there are doubts about a child's safety, the police should be called. You should not place yourself in danger.

If you notice unusual behaviour, for example, a child behaving distractedly after access weekends, you should keep notes of this and follow school or departmental guidelines. The school's lawyers, your union or the education department may provide advice. Make sure that in your notes you do not record opinions but only facts and observations, for example, 'David seems nervous and upset today', not 'David's father has mistreated him again'. The notes should be made part of the official school records.

Family violence orders and stalking

Where a parent has been violent towards, or has harassed or molested, a spouse or child, there may be:
- a Magistrate's Court intervention order (in some states called an 'apprehended violence' or 'protection' order)
- an anti-stalking order
- a Family Court injunction or restraining order
- a Federal Circuit Court injunction or restraining order.

The order can forbid the aggressor from having contact with that family member or from being in a particular place, for example, the area of the school. The police can arrest someone who breaches an injunction or intervention order.

As with parenting orders, it is advisable for a school to sight and copy an intervention order. Then the school has grounds for not releasing the student to the parent. These sorts of disputes should be handled at principal or assistant principal level. If a parent is attempting to breach an intervention order, the police should be contacted immediately. (Bail conditions and good behaviour bonds imposed by courts can also restrict access to schools.)

Where a parent confides in a teacher about violence in the home, the teacher could advise the parent to contact the police, a solicitor or a local community legal centre. If the violence involves the child, then the teacher will have a responsibility under the mandatory reporting laws, and the duty of care, to take action (see 'Reporting child abuse', p. 126).

Name changes

Where divorced parents cannot agree on what the child's name should be, the court can make an order resolving the issue. If a school is caught in a dispute and no order has yet been made, the easiest practice is to use the birth certificate name until the court makes a ruling. Children (like adults) can ask that they be known by another name, but cannot formally change their name until they are 18.

Giving evidence in parenting disputes

Where parents cannot agree on parenting arrangements and the matter is to be decided by the Family Court, a teacher may be asked to give evidence. This may be in the form of a sworn affidavit (a written statement), or teachers may be subpoenaed to give sworn evidence in court (see 'Appearing in court', p. 144).

You do not have to volunteer information regarding family law matters or make an affidavit if you do not want to, but failure to give evidence in court if a subpoena has been served is an offence.

If you receive a subpoena, you should seek advice from the principal regarding departmental or school guidelines about attending court. The party who has issued the subpoena should provide travel expenses.

If a subpoena requests you to bring to court documents relevant to the child, you can only produce documents that are your personal property, unless the school agrees to you taking the official school file. It is not good practice for you to keep personal notes—notes should be placed in the official file and not kept as your personal property (see 'Freedom of information', p. 101).

The school may be served with a subpoena requiring the production of school documents, which will be a matter for the school principal.

Family law problems

CHECKLIST

- ☑ Both parents have legal control of a child unless a court orders otherwise.
- ☑ Step-parents only acquire legal control over a child if the court makes such an order.
- ☑ When children are reluctant to go with a parent, the principal or assistant principal should deal with the matter.
- ☑ Whenever possible, schools should sight and copy court orders relating to parental contact with children. Make sure that the court document you see contains the court seal.
- ☑ You owe a duty of care for your students' safety. If you believe a child is in danger, contact the police.

POLICE INTERVIEWING OF STUDENTS

Teachers can be involved with police interviews where:
- they have been a witness to a crime
- a student has witnessed a crime or is suspected of having committed a crime, and the teacher is present at the interview as an independent person (see 'Interviewing suspects', p. 141).

Interviews may take place at school (if the principal consents) or at the police station. The police can only compel someone to attend a police station if the person is under arrest.

A young person is required to give their name and address where:
- the police have a reasonable belief that they have committed an offence (including on public transport, or drinking in public), or can assist police in investigating a crime
- they are in charge of a motor vehicle involved in an accident (but they do not have to make statements about who caused the accident, or who is at fault)
- they are on a licensed premises where they can also be asked to produce identification to establish that they are not underage.

In other circumstances, young people, like adults, are not required to answer police questions.

A child under 10 cannot be convicted of a crime.

Interviewing suspects

It is always preferable for someone to obtain legal advice before a police interview, or to have a lawyer present at an interview, especially if a serious crime is alleged. For information on the availability of legal assistance and for information on the conduct of police interviews, contact a community legal centre or your state or territory legal aid office (see 'Directory', p. 159).

Police may not interview a young person (under 17 in Queensland, under 18 in other states and territories) who is suspected of having committed a crime unless certain conditions are met. These include providing an opportunity for the student to communicate with their parent, guardian or an independent person, and to have an adult present at the police interview.

You might be asked by a student or their parents to be the independent person at a police interview. If the request comes from the student, you should discuss the matter first with the student's parent or guardian. If the parent or guardian cannot attend or refuses to attend the police interview, then it is appropriate for you to attend. You should also discuss the matter with a senior staff member responsible for student welfare.

Role of an independent person

The independent person in a police interview does not act as advocate. Their role is to provide support for the young person, to witness the interview and, by their presence, discourage overbearing behaviour from the police. In particular, an independent person should:
- make detailed notes of how long the student has been held, the conduct of the interview and any concerns about their treatment. It may be necessary to intervene if the student's rights are being infringed
- speak privately with the student and make sure they understand the purpose of the interview, find out

if they have complaints about their treatment and ascertain whether an interpreter is required
- check that the police are observing proper procedures and that the student understands that they have the right not to answer any police questions
- be present if fingerprints are taken. Young people may be fingerprinted, although in some states and territories a court order might be required depending on the age and capacity of the child, and parental and child consent
- bring to the attention of police any instances of the student being unwell or confused.

Interviewing victims and witnesses

Where a student who is a victim or who has witnessed a crime is to be interviewed by the police, it is appropriate for a teacher to be present to offer support. The student's parent or guardian should be notified that the police want to interview the student (unless the matter relates to alleged parental abuse).

Students who are victims of crimes might be eligible for financial assistance through a victims of crime compensation scheme.

Teacher as witness

A teacher interviewed as a witness where a student is the criminal suspect is in the same position as any other witness. While it is a civic duty to assist police with the investigation of crime, witnesses are not required to answer any self-incriminating questions (that is, questions where the answer might suggest that you have committed a crime). Any evidence given to the police can be used in court later.

If you are not sure what to do, you should seek advice from a lawyer, union or the education department before the interview, and tell police you would like to delay the interview until you have had that advice.

> **CHECKLIST**
>
> ☑ Where students are accused of crimes, advise them to obtain legal representation, particularly if it is a serious crime.
>
> ☑ Contact the student's parents or guardian unless the matter relates to alleged parental abuse.
>
> ☑ There are rules governing police interviewing procedures where a young person is suspected of having committed a crime.
>
> ☑ You may act as a student's independent person at a police interview. An independent person's role is to support the student, to witness and note how interviews are conducted, and to see whether the process is understood. Take factual notes as a record for future reference.
>
> ☑ There is a right not to answer self-incriminating questions.

APPEARING IN COURT

Giving character evidence

The most common situation in which character evidence is required is in a criminal case where a student has pleaded guilty to a crime or has been found guilty of a crime. To help the judge or magistrate decide on an appropriate sentence, the defence may call on professional reports (e.g. from a psychiatrist, psychologist or social worker), or character witnesses (e.g. from a teacher).

Character evidence is given in court under oath. It is an offence to lie under oath. The defence lawyer will ask questions about the student, such as their behaviour and performance at school in all activities, abilities, relationships with peers and family, and any information teachers have about out-of-school activities and interests. Sometimes the judge or magistrate will also ask a question. A character witness is not usually cross-examined by the prosecution.

Be careful if asked to provide a character reference (which will be considered before sentencing) for a fellow teacher convicted of a criminal offence, particularly if the offence relates to grooming or other child abuse. Both the headmaster and leading teacher at a private school in Melbourne were required to stand down by the school community after they provided references for a teacher convicted of a grooming offence.[1]

Giving evidence in a contested case

There are many cases—criminal, civil, welfare and family law—in which teachers could be asked to give sworn evidence in court about what they have observed. For example, the teacher might have to give evidence if an injured student sues the school for negligence. In a family law dispute, you might be required to report on the child's academic progress, emotional state and behaviour in school with peers and parents.

If the school is reluctant to give you time off school to attend court, explain this to the lawyer who wants you to attend, and a subpoena can then be served on you (see 'Giving evidence in parenting disputes', p. 138).

You will be asked questions by the lawyer for the party that called you. Unlike giving character evidence, giving evidence in a contested case will involve you being cross-examined by the lawyer for the opposing party. This can be a rigorous process, as a cross-examining lawyer attempts to find any doubts or inconsistencies in a witness's evidence.

A witness's role is to give truthful and unbiased answers to all questions. You cannot be sued for defamation for anything you say when giving evidence in court.

CHECKLIST

- ☑ You can be called to give character evidence or evidence about the disputed facts of a case.
- ☑ If you are served a subpoena, you must attend court.
- ☑ The role of the witness is to provide factual information based on observations, not to advise the court.
- ☑ Not telling the truth under oath is an offence.

TRESPASS ON SCHOOL PROPERTY

Schools (including government schools) are not places open to the general public—they occupy either private or Crown land and no one has a right to be on the school premises. Consequently, any person who is on school property without permission and who remains after being asked to leave is trespassing. The principal, or any staff member acting with the principal's authority, can ask someone to leave.

If a trespasser refuses to leave, the police should be called. It would be unwise for a staff member to attempt to forcibly eject someone from the property, because those actions may amount to an assault. If someone is a persistent trespasser, or behaves in a threatening manner, a court order can be obtained forbidding them from entering school property.

As it is known that school grounds are often used without permission by the general public (especially children) after school hours for recreation, the school has a responsibility to ensure that the school premises and equipment (play equipment, goal rings, etc.) are in safe condition (see 'Duty of care', p. 5).

Who has permission to be there?

All visitors to a school must present at the school's administration office and register as an authorised visitor. The school should have a record of who is on the premises at any one time. This is particularly important if there is an emergency.

The following people have permission to be on school property:
- staff
- students
- parents at the school to see staff or to drop off or collect their children
- someone with a reason to visit the school (e.g. a representative of an educational publishing company, a tradesperson, a student coming from another school for sport). The school should check that regular visitors have a Working With Children Check
- anybody that has entered into a contract with the school to use school facilities (e.g. the school rents out its hall to a community organisation for a function). The right of entry is limited to the area specified in the agreement and is governed by the terms and conditions of the contract.

Parents are not entitled to wander about the school without permission unless the school's policy is to permit this. Parents who wish to see their children during class time, or to collect their children before the day finishes should first go to the school's administration office where they may need to sign the child out (see 'Family law problems', p. 134).

Other persons may approach the general office to indicate why they wish to visit the school, but they may not wander around the school without permission.

Strangers

There have been many instances of assaults and sexual offences committed by unauthorised people coming onto school property. You should question any stranger found in the school grounds, and if a satisfactory explanation for their presence is not given, the person should be asked to leave and the matter reported immediately to the school administration. Again, if a trespasser refuses to leave, the police should be called, rather than staff attempting to forcibly eject the trespasser.

CHECKLIST

- Schools are private property.
- Anyone who refuses to leave the property when requested to is a trespasser.
- People not normally on the school premises should first report to the administration office for permission to be at the school.
- The police should be called if a trespasser refuses to leave.
- A court order can be obtained preventing someone who is threatening or a nuisance from entering school property.

NOTES

DUTY OF CARE
1. *Doulis v. State of Victoria* (2014) VSC 395
2. *The Trustees of the Roman Catholic Church for the Diocese of Bathurst v. Koffman and Anor* (1996) NSWSC 346
3. *Reynolds v. Haines* (unreported, New South Wales Supreme Court, BC9305229, 27 October 1993)
4. *Geyer v. Downes* (1977) ALR 408
5. *St Mark's Orthodox Coptic College v. Abraham* (2007) NSWCA 185
6. *Barker v. State of South Australia* (1978) 19 SASR
7. *Johns v. Minister of Education* (1981) 28 SASR 206
8. *Commonwealth v. Introvigne* (1982) 150 CLR 258
9. *Inquest into the deaths of Hannah Taylor and Amelia Catherine McGuiness* (2011) NSWLC 13
10. McCrory, P et al., 'Consensus statement on concussion in sport: the 4th International Conference on Concussion in Sport held in Zurich, November 2012', British Journal of Sports Medicine, vol. 47, no. 5, 2013, pp. 250–8. bjsm.bmj.com/content/47/5/250.full.pdf+html
11. 'Consensus statement on concussion in sport: the 5th international Conference on Concussion in Sport held in Berlin, April 28 2017'. https://completeconcussions.com/2017/04/28/consensus-statement-concussion-sport/
12. *Nicholas v. Osborne & ors* (unreported, Victoria County Court, November 1985)
13. *Diocese of Canberra and Goulburn v. Farrah Hadba* (2005) HCA 31 at 25
14. *Harvey v. Pennell & the State of South Australia* (1987) 46 SASR 83

EXCURSIONS AND CAMPS
1. Coroners Court of New South Wales, *Inquest into the death of David Iredale*, Penrith, 2009. www.coroners.lawlink.nsw.gov.au/agdbasev7wr/_assets/coroners/m401601I6/62_iredalefindings.pdf
2. *Harris v. Trustees of the Roman Catholic Church for the Archdiocese of Sydney* (2011) NSWDC 172, confirmed on appeal in Perisher Blue Pty Limited v. Harris (2013) NSWCA 38. http://www6.austlii.edu.au/cgi-bin/viewdoc/au/cases/nsw/NSWDC/2011/172.html?stem=0&synonyms=0&query=title(harris%20)&nocontext=1 (See also a recent case from the UK, *Woodland v. Essex County Council* (2013) UKSC 66. 26.)

Notes

FIRST AID AND DISEASE
1. Coroners Court of Victoria, *Inquest into the death of Nathan Fazal Francis*, Melbourne, 1 June 2012.

STUDENT DISCIPLINE AND RESTRAINT
1. *Moran v. Victorian Institute of Teachers* (2007) s. 85, VCAT 1311. www.austlii.edu.au/au/cases/vic/VCAT/2007/1311.html
2. Victorian Consolidated Regulations, *Education and Training Reform Regulations, 2017-REG 25*. 'Restraint from danger'. http://classic.austlii.edu.au/au/legis/vic/consol_reg/eatrr2017382/s25.html
3. McKenna, K, 'RTI documents reveal allegations of abuse by state education teaching staff against students with disability', *ABC*, 4 November 2019. https://www.abc.net.au/news/2019-11-04/rti-student-abuse-allegations-against-state-education-staff/11667674
4. McKenna, K, 'Education Queensland sued by boy with ADHD after school restrains him over "aggressive" acts', *ABC*, 28 August 2019. https://www.abc.net.au/news/2019-08-28/boy-with-adhd-suing-education-queensland-restraint-isolation/11453644
5. Fry, H, 'After autistic boy dies during school restraint, 3 educators charged with manslaughter', *Los Angeles Times*, 13 November 2019. https://www.latimes.com/california/story/2019-11-13/autistic-boy-dies-school-restraint-educators-charged-manslaughter
6. *NN v. Tunkhannock Area School District et al.*, 10-cv-01080-ARC. (See also www.aclu.org/free-speech/aclu-settle-student-cell-phonesearch-lawsuit-northeast-pennsylvania-school-district)
7. Law Reform Committee, *Report of the Law Reform Committee for the Inquiry into Sexting*, Parl. Paper 230, Parliament of Victoria, East Melbourne, May 2013. www.parliament.vic.gov.au/images/stories/committees/lawrefrom/isexting/LRC_Sexting_Final_Report.pdf
8. Tallon, K, Choi, A, Keeley, M, Elliott, J & Maher, J, *New voices/new laws: school-age young people in New South Wales speak out about the criminal laws that apply to their online behaviour*, National Children's and Youth Law Centre & Legal Aid, New South Wales, 2012. www.lawstuff.org.au/__data/assets/pdf_file/0009/15030/New-Voices-Law-Reform-Report.pdf
9. *Crimes Act 1958 S51M inserted by No 47/2016 S16.*
10. *Criminal Legislation Amendment (Child Sexual Abuse) Act 2018 No 33*
11. Department of Justice, *Intimate Image Abuse in Western Australia*, WA, March 2021. https://www.wa.gov.au/government/publications/intimate-image-abuse-western-australia

Notes

PHYSICAL CONTACT AND SEXUAL ASSAULT
1. *Horan v. Ferguson* (1995) 2 QD R 490
2. Macdonald, E, 'Teacher student sex - laws under the microscope', *The Canberra Times*, 8 May 2015. https://www.canberratimes.com.au/story/6067954/teacher-student-sex-laws-under-the-microscope/ ; Hamilton Smith, L, 'Queensland carnal knowledge laws labelled "archaic" by legal reform expert after teacher acquitted', *ABC*, 24 June 2019. https://www.abc.net.au/news/2019-06-24/queensland-laws-on-teacher-student-sex/11229092
3. *Withyman v. State of New South Wales & Blackburn* (2010) NSWDC 186
4. *Withyman v. State of New South Wales & Blackburn; Blackburn v. Withyman* (2013) NSWCA 10
5. *Crimes Amendment (Grooming) Act 2014*
6. Jacks, T, 'Brotherly bond or grooming?', *The Age*, 8 April 2017. https://www.theage.com.au/national/victoria/brotherly-bond-or-child-abuse-plot-historic-case-challenges-new-grooming-law-20170408-gvgmtw.html

BULLYING, HARASSMENT AND ASSAULT
1. *Gregory v. State of New South Wales* (2009) NSWSC 559
2. Tomazin, F, 'Bullied teenager gets $290,000 in settlement', *The Age*, 11 March 2010. www.theage.com.au/victoria/bullied-teenager-gets-290000-in-settlement-20100310-pz9o.html
3. *Oyston v St Patrick's College* (2013) NSWCA 135
4. Ibid at 146.

DISCRMINATION
1. *Hurst v. State of Queensland* (2006) FCAFC 100; 151 FCR 562; 235 ALR 53; 91 ALD 575
2. Gallo, L, 'Prestigious school forced to apologise to autistic girl's family', *WA today*, 21 December 2010. https://www.watoday.com.au/national/western-australia/prestigious-school-forced-to-apologise-to-autistic-girls-family-20101221-1940f.html
3. *Finney v The Hills Grammar School* (1999) HREOCA
4. *Walker v State of Victoria* (2011) FCA
5. *Connor v State of Queensland (Department of Education and Training) (No 3)* (2020) FCA
6. *Sex Discrimination Act 1984 S42*
7. *Taylor and Others v Moorabbin Saints Junior Football League and Football Victoria Ltd* (2004) VCAT 158

Notes

CONFIDENTIALITY, PRIVACY AND FREEDOM OF INFORMATION
1. OAIC, 'Australian Privacy Principles and National Privacy Principles: comparison guide', Canberra, 2013. www.oaic.gov.au/privacy/privacyresources/privacy-guides/australian-privacy-principles-and-nationalprivacy-principles-comparison-guide
2. Independent Schools Council of Australia & National Catholic Education Commission, *Privacy compliance manual*, ISCA, 2013. www.isca.edu.au/wp-content/uploads/2011/03/Privacy-Compliance-Manual-Amended-September-2013.pdf

DEFAMATION
1. Santo, M, 'Australian principal wins $40,000 award after Facebook hate page created', *Examiner*, 21 December 2012. www.examiner.com/article/australian-principal-wins-40-000-award-after-hate-facebookpage-created
2. *Mickle v Farley* (2013) NSWDC 295 (29 November 2013)
3. *Brose v Baluskas & Ors (No 6)* (2020) QDC 15

COPYRIGHT
1. *The Copyright Amendment (Disability Access and Other Measures) Act 2017*
2. Australian Copyright Council, *Notices on photocopiers & other copying equipment*, Strawberry Hills, January 2014. www.copyright.org.au
3. National Copyright Unit, *What is Creative Commons?*, Parramatta, 2021. https://smartcopying.edu.au/what-is-creative-commons/
4. Department of Infrastructure, Transport, Regional Development and Communications, 'Copyright access reforms', Department of Infrastructure, Transport, Regional Development and Communications, Canberra, 13 August 2020. https://www.communications.gov.au/departmental-news/copyright-access-reforms
5. Copyright Agency, *Online teaching and Covid-19*, Copyright Agency, 8 April 2020. https://www.copyright.com.au/licences-permission/educational-licences/online-teaching/

REPORTING CHILD ABUSE
1. *Crimes Act 1958 S490*. http://classic.austlii.edu.au/au/legis/vic/consol_act/ca195882/s49o.html

APPEARING IN COURT
1. Milligan, L, Gartry, L, staff, 'St Kevin's College headmaster resigns over grooming scandal', *The New Daily*, 19 February 2020. https://thenewdaily.com.au/news/state/vic/2020/02/19/st-kevins-headmaster-resigns/

FURTHER READING

Butler D and Matthews B (2007) *Schools and the law*, The Federation Press, Sydney.

Edwards J, Ford D, Knott A, Shorten A, Stewart D and Verma R (eds) (2013) *Hands on guide: school principals legal guide*, CCH Australia, Sydney.

Edwards J, Knott A and Riley D (1997) *Australian schools and the law*, LBC Information Services, Sydney.

Jackson J and Varnham S (2007) *Law for educators: school and university law in Australia*, LexisNexis Butterworths, Chatswood.

Ramsay I and Shorten A (1996) *Education and the law*, Butterworths, Sydney.

Stewart D and Knott A (2002), *Schools, courts and the law: managing student welfare*, Prentice Hall, Sydney.

DIRECTORY

General contacts

Australia and New Zealand Law Association (ANZELA)
Publishes the *International Journal of Law and Education* and holds an annual conference on law and education.
Website: www.anzela.edu.au

Australian Copyright Council
Provides online legal advice for schools in all states except Queensland.
245 Chalmers St, Redfern NSW 2016
PO Box 1986, Strawberry Hills, NSW 2012
Telephone: (02) 9101 2377
Email: info@copyright.org.au
Website: www.copyright.org.au

Australian Education Union
See the federal website for state-specific branches.
Federal Office
120 Clarendon St, Southbank VIC 3006
Phone: (03) 9693 1800
Facsimile: (03) 9693 1805
Email: aeu@aeufederal.org.au
Website: www.aeufederal.org.au

Australian Legal Information Institute (AustLII)
Provides free online legal information (including both primary legal material from federal, state and territory jurisdictions and secondary legal material created by public bodies) plus other national and international links.
Website: www.austlii.edu.au

Directory

Australasian Mechanical Copyright Owners Society (AMCOS)
Managed by APRA—see contact details below.

Australasian Performing Rights Association (APRA)
See website for state-specific contact details.
Website: https://apraamcos.com.au

Australian Recording Industry Association (ARIA)
Website: www.aria.com.au

Copyright Agency Limited (CAL)
Level 12, 66 Goulburn St, Sydney NSW 2000
Toll free (within Australia): 1800 066 844
Telephone: (02) 9394 7600
Fax: (02) 9394 7601
Website: www.copyright.com.au

Disability Standards for Education
Australian Government Department of Education
Website: www.education.gov.au/disability-standards-education

Education Services Australia
For access to digital learning resources
Website: https://www.esa.edu.au/

Family Court of Australia
Offices in each capital city (except Perth, where the State Family Court of Western Australia should be contacted) and some regions.
National Enquiry Centre
GPO Box 9991, Parramatta NSW 2150
Phone: 1300 352 000
Website: www.familycourt.gov.au

Federal Circuit Court of Australia
(Formerly Federal Magistrates' Court of Australia.)
Shares facilities with the Family Court.
Website: www.federalcircuitcourt.gov.au

Human Rights Commission
Level 3, 175 Pitt Street, Sydney NSW 2001
GPO Box 5218, Sydney NSW 2001
General enquiries: 1300 369 711
Complaints: 1300 656 419
Email: infoservice@humanrights.gov.au
Website: www.humanrights.gov.au
(Provides links to state and territory organisations.)

Lawstuff
A useful site for information on young people and the law.
Website: www.lawstuff.org.au

National Association of Community Legal Centres (NACLC)
Peak body representing community legal centres, which are independent community-based, government-funded organisations. NACLC provides free legal advice and advocacy across a wide range of areas of law.
Website: www.naclc.org.au

National Legal Aid
Website provides links to state and territory legal aid commissions.
GPO Box 1422, Hobart TAS 7001
Website: www.nationallegalaid.org

Office of the Australian Information Commissioner (OAIC)
Independent Australian Government agency established under the *Australian Information Commissioner Act 2010* concerned with privacy, freedom of information and government information policy.

Directory

GPO Box 5218, Sydney NSW 2001
Telephone: 1300 363 992
Email: enquiries@oaic.gov.au
Website: www.oaic.gov.au

Screenrights (Audio-Visual Copyright Society Ltd)
Level 1, 140 Myrtle Street, Chippendale NSW 2008
PO Box 853, Broadway NSW 2007
Telephone: (02) 8038 1300
Email: info@screenrights.org
Website: www.screenrights.org

Smartcopying
The official guide to copyright issues for Australian schools and TAFE colleges.
Website: www.smartcopying.edu.au
Useful information sheets for schools can be accessed at https://www.smartcopying.edu.au/information-sheets/schools

Bullying

Cyber Safety in Schools

Education Services Australia
Website: https://www.esa.edu.au

eSafety Commissioner
Website: https://www.esafety.gov.au

National Framework for Values Education in Australian Schools
Website: http://www.curriculum.edu.au/values/val_national_framework_for_values_education,8757.html

National Safe Schools Framework
2013 revision
Website: http://www.educationcouncil.edu.au/site/
DefaultSite/filesystem/documents/Reports%20
and%20publications/Publications/Safe%20school%20
environment/National_safe_schools_framework_(2013_
Update).pdf

Student Wellbeing Hub
Website: https://studentwellbeinghub.edu.au/

Child protection
To report a case of actual or suspected child abuse, contact the relevant community services department.

Australian Capital Territory
Office for Children, Youth and Family Support
Mandated reporters: 1300 556 728
General public: 1300 556 729 (also after hours)
Website: https://www.accesscanberra.act.gov.au/app/
answers/detail/a_id/213/~/reporting-child-abuse-and-
neglect

New South Wales
Department of Family and Community Services
Mandated reporters: 13 21 11
Child Abuse Prevention Services (CAPS): 1800 688 009
DoCS helpline: 13 21 11 (24-hour child protection service)
Website: www.community.nsw.gov.au

Northern Territory
Family and Children's Services
Telephone: 1800 700 250 (24 hours)
Website: https://nt.gov.au/law/crime/report-child-abuse

Directory

Queensland
Child Safety Services
Telephone: 1800 811 810 (business hours)
Telephone: 1800 177 135 (after hours)
Website: www.communities.qld.gov.au/childsafety/about-us/contact-us
https://www.csyw.qld.gov.au/child-family/protecting-children/reporting-child-abuse

South Australia
Department for Education and Child Development
Telephone: 13 14 78 (24 hours)
Website: https://www.sa.gov.au/topics/education-and-learning/health-wellbeing-and-special-needs/report-child-abuse/report-child-abuse

Tasmania
Department of Health and Human Services
Advice and referral line: 1800 000 123
Child Protection Service: 1300 737 639 (24 hours)
Child and Family Services: 1800 001 219 (24 hours)
Website: https://www.health.tas.gov.au/contact/child_protection_notification_form

Victoria
Department of Human Services
Child Protection Emergency Service: 13 12 78 (after hours)
For local district contact details, see website.
Website: https://services.dhhs.vic.gov.au/reporting-child-abuse

Western Australia
Department for Child Protection and Family Support
Mandated reporters: 1800 708 704
Central intake team: 1800 273 889
Crisis Care Helpline
Telephone: (08) 9223 1111 (24 hours)
Toll free: 1800 199 008
For local district office contact details, see website.
Website: https://mandatoryreporting.dcp.wa.gov.au/Pages/DCP_DistrictOffices.aspx

INDEX

age and sport discrimination 92
anaphylaxis 40–2, 97
anti-discrimination laws 54, 73, 82, 84–5
artistic works and copyright 114–20
assault 54, 72–8
   see also sexual assault
asthma 43
Australian Copyright Council 112, 116, 121
Australian Institute for Teaching and School Leadership (AITSL) 2
Australian Privacy Principles (APP) 97, 98
Australian Professional Standards for Teachers 2–3
Australian Society of Clinical Immunology (ASCIA) 40, 41, 42

bag searches 57
blood spills 39
bring your own device (BYOD) 17, 76
bullying 72–8
   cyberbullying 9, 12, 17, 61, 73, 75–6
   definition 72–3
   legal remedies 73–4
   policies 74–5

cable programs and copyright 116
camps 25–31
   clothing and weather 29–30
   day and higher risk category 28
   day and lower risk category 28
   duty of care 9, 13, 25
   emergency planning 29
   health care and first aid 29
   overnight and higher risk category 28
   planning and risk assessment 26–30
   run by other organisations 25–6
   use of your own car 30
character evidence 144
child abuse, reporting 95, 126–33, 137
   Child Safe Principles 132
   and confidentiality 131
   consequences of reporting 131
   failure to protect 132
   how to report 127
   mandated reporting 126, 128–30
   National Office for Child Safety 132
   reasonable grounds 126–7, 128–30, 131
   Royal Commission into Institutional Responses to Child Sex Abuse 131–2
child pornography 60–1
Child Safe Principles 132
confidential information from students 95–102
confidentiality 39, 97–100, 102, 131
   see also privacy
confiscations 63
copyright 112–23
   Australian Copyright Council 112, 114, 116, 119
   computer programs 117
   Copyright Agency Limited (CAL) 113
   COVID-19, impact of 121–2
   Creative Commons 120
   and disabilities 119
   for educational purposes 113–20
   electronic form material 114–20
   expiry 113
   films 117
   format-shifting 118
   moral rights 114, 116
   music 115
   National Copyright Guidelines 112
   ownership 112
   performing 115
   printed material 114–20
   streaming services 117
   and students 119–20
   television, cable and radio 116
   video hosting sites 117
   websites, creating 113
corporal punishment 52–3
court appearances 138, 144–5
   duty of care 12, 96
   giving character evidence 144
   giving evidence in a contested case 145
court orders (family law) 135–6
COVID-19 45–6, 76, 121–2
Creative Commons 120
criminal record check (CRC) 3
Critical Incidents Policy 45
cyberbullying 9, 12, 17, 61, 75–6

Index

defamation 103–8
    damage to reputation 103
    defences to 104–6
    and innuendo 103–4
    and school publications and productions 106–7
    and social media 103, 107
direct discrimination 86
disabilities and copyright 119
disability standards for education 88–90
discipline 52–64
    confiscation 63
    corporal punishment 52–3
    discrimination 53
    drug testing 62
    government schools 52
    non-government schools 52
    restraint 54–7
    ridicule and humiliation 54
    scope of your powers 53
    searches 57
    sexting 60–1
discrimination 82–94
    direct and indirect 86–7
    disability standards for education 88–90
    and discipline 54
    exemptions for schools 84–5
    grounds of 82–4
    and infectious diseases 39, 83
    and sexual harassment 92–3
    and sport 91
disease 38–44
drug testing 62
Duke of Edinburgh scheme 25
duty of care 5–24, 38, 95
    apologies 23
    before and after school 10–11
    common practices 18–19
    court appearances 12, 96, 138
    and family law problems 136
    and first aid 38
    foreseeable events 15–16
    and health conditions 40–3
    how careful do you have to be? 14–15
    and infectious diseases 39
    and injuries 22–3, 54–7
    legal protection for employees 7
    non-government schools 8–9
    and non-teaching staff 32–4
    online learning activities 11–12
    playground supervision 10, 16, 20–1
    and professional negligence 109
    professional standards 18
    school events 12
    school's 7–8, 136
    and sexting 60–1
    and social media 17–18
    and sport 17, 18, 21–2
    student injuries 22–3
    student:teacher ratios and guidelines 19, 27
    teachers with specialist skills 19
    and trainee teachers 32–3
    what to do if you are being sued 14
    when is it owed? 9–10
    who is liable? teacher or school? 12–14
DVDs and copyright 118

Education and Training Reform Regulations 2017 55
evidence
    giving evidence in a contested case 145
excursions 25–31
    clothing and weather 29–30
    day and higher risk category 28
    day and lower risk category 28–9
    duty of care 9, 13, 25
    emergency planning 29
    health care and first aid 29
    overnight and higher risk category 28
    planning and risk assessment 26–8
    run by other organisations 25–6
    use of your own car 30

Facebook 70, 75, 107
failure to protect
family law problems 134–9
    court orders 135–6
    family violence orders 137
    giving evidence in parenting disputes 138
    name changes 137–8
    school reports, notices and excursions 135
    school's duty of care 136
    stalking 137
    when disputes arise 134
    who has legal control over a child? 134
family violence orders 137
first aid 22, 29, 32–3, 38–44
    administering 32–3, 38–9
    anaphylaxis 40–2
    asthma 43
    duty of care 38–9
    and health conditions 40–3

Index

and non-teaching staff 32–3
format-shifting and copyright 118–19
freedom of Information 96, 101–2

gender identity and discrimination 83, 85, 86
government schools
  and discipline 52
  and drug testing 62
  and privacy 96–7
grooming 12, 13, 48, 68, 77, 144

harassment 54, 72–8
  definition 72
  legal remedies 73–4
  policies 74–5, 93
  sexual 92–3
  of students with disabilities 90
  of teachers 77–8
health and safety laws 56
health conditions
  anaphylaxis 40–2
  asthma 43
  duty of care 40–3
  and legal responsibility 40–3
humiliation 53, 54

impairment and sport discrimination 91
inappropriate relationships 68–9
indirect discrimination 87
injuries
  caused by other students 23
  duty of care 22, 54–7
  school's liability for students 36
  student fault 23
  volunteers 36
internet
  and bullying 75, 77
  and copyright 118
  duty of care 17–8, 76–7
  and safety 76–7
  and sexting 60, 61

learning difficulties, identifying (professional negligence) 110
learning disabilities 90
locker searches 57

material safety data sheets (MSDS) 32
medications, administering 39–40
mobile phones 58–60, 60–2
moral rights and copyright 114, 116
music and copyright 115

National Copyright Guidelines 112

National Disability Insurance Scheme (NDIS) 88
National Office for Child Safety 132
National Privacy Principles (NPP) 97–8
negligence *see* professional negligence
non-government schools
  and discipline 52
  and drug testing 62
  duty of care 8–9
  and privacy 97–100, 101
non-teaching staff 32–4

occupational health and safety legislation 13–14
online learning 11–12, 47–9, 76–7, 121–2

pandemics 45–9
  COVID-19 45, 46
  Critical Incidents Policy 45
  hygiene 45
  and online learning 47–9, 121–2
  quarantine and self-isolation 45–6
  and school closures 46
people with disabilities and copyright 119
performing rights and copyright 115–16
physical contact (teacher/student) 13, 30, 54–7, 65–71
physical education, duty of care 20, 21–2
playground supervision, duty of care 10–11, 16, 20–1
police interviewing of students 140–3
principals and duty of care 9, 11, 40–1, 132, 136–7
printed material and copyright 114–20
privacy 96–101
  and consent 97, 99, 100
  government schools 96–7
  non-government schools 97–100
  notifiable data breaches 97
  Office of the Australian Information Commissioner (OAIC) 97
  photographs, and consent 100
  Privacy Amendment Act 97
  and student's rights 100–1
professional negligence 109–11
punishment 52, 53
  corporal 52–3

radio programs and copyright 116–17
restraint 16, 54–7
  see also discipline, ridicule and humiliation 54

Index

Royal Commission into Institutional Responses to Child Sex Abuse 131–3

searches 57
sex discrimination and sport 91
sexting 17, 59, 60–2, 67
sexual abuse 126–7
sexual assault 13, 30, 54–7, 57, 65–71
   Facebook 70
   inappropriate relationships 68–9
   'grooming' a child under 16 68
   touching students 65–6
sexual contact with students 66–8
sexual harassment 92–3
Smartcopying 112
social media 17–18, 70, 75, 100
sport and discrimination 91
sport and duty of care 17, 18, 21–2
stalking 72, 73, 75, 137
strangers and trespass on school property 147–8
streaming services and copyright 117
student's rights (privacy) 100–1
student:teacher ratios and guidelines (duty of care) 19

teacher registration and professional standards 2–4
TeacherTube and copyright 117
television programs and copyright 116–17
trespass on school property 146–8

USBs (storage devices) and copyright 118

Victorian Civil and Administrative Tribunal (VCAT) 54, 84
video hosting sites and copyright 117
volunteers 27, 35–7, 93, 100, 126

websites and copyright 113
working with children check (WWC Check) 3, 26, 35, 147

YouTube and copyright 117